The OS X Mountain Lion **Pocket**Guide

Jeff**Carlson**

Ginormous knowledge, pocket sized.

Peachpit Press

The OS X Mountain Lion Pocket Guide
Jeff Carlson

Peachpit Press
1249 Eighth Street
Berkeley, CA 94710
510/524-2178
510/524-2221 (fax)

Find us on the Web at: www.peachpit.com
To report errors, please send a note to errata@peachpit.com

Peachpit Press is a division of Pearson Education.

Editor: Clifford Colby
Copyeditor: Scout Festa
Production editor: David Van Ness
Compositor: Jeff Carlson
Indexer: Valerie Haynes Perry
Cover design: Peachpit Press
Interior design: Peachpit Press

ISBN-13:   978-0-321-85713-2
ISBN-10:   0-321-85713-5

9 8 7 6 5 4 3 2 1

Printed and bound in the United States of America

For Kim Ricketts

Acknowledgments

You probably have an image in your head of a book writer: holed up in an attic office space, alone, sleep-deprived, heading downstairs occasionally for coffee and sugar and the stray bit of protein. Well, yeah, that's pretty much true. However, I wasn't alone. Physically alone at times, but always connected to a fantastic group of people who helped make it possible and who have my thanks:

Glenn Fleishman wrote the original versions of chapters 8 and 10 for the Snow Leopard edition of this book, when I realized that it wasn't possible to clone myself.

My editorial team provided every resource I needed: Cliff Colby at Peachpit Press; my copyeditor Scout Festa; my production editor David Van Ness; and my indexer Valerie Perry.

Teresa Brewer, Janette Barrios, Monica Sarkar, Jennie Syme, and Keri Walker at Apple answered my questions and provided review equipment for my *Seattle Times* column, which indirectly aided the creation of this book.

My friends Andrew Laurence and Agen G. N. Schmitz let me bounce around ideas at all hours and helped with some technical questions.

Kim Carlson and Eliana Carlson brought me joy (and candy!) as I juggled the roles of husband, father, and author on a tight timeline.

About Jeff Carlson

Jeff Carlson gave up an opportunity to intern at a design firm during college because they really just wanted someone tall to play on their volleyball team. In the intervening years, he's been a designer and writer, authoring best-selling books on the Macintosh, Web design, video editing, and photography. He's currently a columnist for the *Seattle Times* and a senior editor of the respected electronic newsletter *TidBITS* (www.tidbits.com), and he consumes almost too much coffee. Almost.

Find more information about him at jeffcarlson.com and neverenoughcoffee.com, and follow him on Twitter at @jeffcarlson.

Contents

Introduction

A lot has happened since Apple introduced OS X a decade ago (then called "Mac OS X"). What started as an incomplete replacement for an established operating system has become not only the backbone of today's powerful Mac computers, but also the foundation for the iPhone, iPad, iPod touch, and Apple TV. At one point, that was just a novel bit of technology trivia, but with OS X Mountain Lion, many capabilities found in those handheld devices are coming back to the desktop.

The signature features of Mountain Lion are inspired by iOS. Several new features that were formerly iOS-only now have Mac counterparts: Notification Center keeps you up to date on current information, Messages lets you use the iMessage service to send text messages—for free—to any iOS device that's also using iMessage, and the Notes and

Reminders apps bring mobile data to your desktop (and back out again). Most importantly, Mountain Lion is the first version of OS X that takes advantage of iCloud, Apple's free service for syncing and sharing data among all your devices. More than just a nifty service to shuttle your contacts and calendar items around, iCloud is turning into an indispensable way to interact with these various computing devices. Being able to edit a document on your Mac and instantly switch to editing it on an iPad or iPhone with all changes intact will make you wonder how we put up with moving data across cables for so long.

With Mountain Lion, Apple is setting up the Mac (and how it interacts with the iOS devices) for the next decade.

How to Get Mountain Lion

If you've just purchased a new Mac, congratulations! Mountain Lion is already installed. If you are upgrading, your options include the following:

- If you're currently running Mac OS X 10.7 Lion or 10.6 Snow Leopard, you can buy Mountain Lion for $19.99 from the Mac App Store and download it; Mountain Lion is not available on disc (see Chapter 2 for more details).

- If you're running Mac OS X 10.5 or earlier, you must first upgrade to Snow Leopard ($29) to gain access to the Mac App Store.

note Snow Leopard users may have an uncomfortable surprise waiting when upgrading to Mountain Lion. Applications that were originally written for PowerPC-based processors will not run at all. With OS X Lion, Apple removed Rosetta, a technology for translating instructions from PowerPC to Intel code. That means any older software you rely on may not make the leap to the new operating system and will require that you purchase new versions or find alternative programs.

Will your Mac run Mountain Lion?

Mountain Lion runs on the following Intel-based Apple computers:

- iMac (Mid 2007 or newer)
- MacBook (Late 2008 Aluminum, or Early 2009 or newer)
- MacBook Pro (Mid/Late 2007 or newer)
- MacBook Air (Late 2008 or newer)
- Mac mini (Early 2009 or newer)
- Mac Pro (Early 2008 or newer)
- Xserve (Early 2009)

If you're not sure which specific Mac model you own, do this:

1. Go to the Apple menu ( ) and choose About This Mac (**Figure i.1**).

Figure i.1
About This Mac

2. Click the More Info button, which launches the System Information application (**Figure i.2**, on the next page). The model is listed beneath the product name.

Figure i.2
More Mac info

Mac model

How Big Is Your Pocket?

I don't cover absolutely every aspect of Mountain Lion in this book; there's just too much information for a Pocket Guide (and none of *my* pockets are large enough to carry a 500-page book). Therefore, I've focused on what I believe are the most important—or just plain cool—elements of Mountain Lion. If you're looking for a more thorough reference, I highly recommend Maria Langer's *OS X Mountain Lion: Visual QuickStart Guide*.

I'm also making some assumptions: You know how to turn on your computer, operate the mouse or trackpad, and take precautions such as not resting open beverages directly on the keyboard (I mean, balancing a martini on the top edge of your iMac is one thing, but keep it away from the keyboard for heaven's sake!).

As this isn't a basic-level guide, I'll also assume that you know some of the core actions of using a computer in the twenty-first century, such as starting up and shutting down your Mac, accessing menu items (single-click a menu name that appears at the top of the screen to reveal its list of options), and double-clicking an application to launch it.

note Actually, I often see people, even experienced users, confused about the difference between clicking and double-clicking items, so here's the deal: Click once to *select* something (such as a document file); double-click the item to *open* it.

Conventions Used in This Book

- When I talk about accessing a command from the menus that appear in every program, I separate each component using an angle bracket (>) character. For example, "choose File > Open" means "Click the File menu item, then choose Open from the list that appears." A succession of commands indicate submenus: "choose View > Arrange By > Name" translates to "click the View menu, then the Arrange By item, and then the Name item in the submenu that appears."

- When I refer to a "preference pane," I'm talking about the options found in System Preferences. Choose System Preferences from the Apple (🍎) menu, or click its icon in the Dock. To access the "Network preference pane," for example, open System Preferences and click the Network icon.

- Keyboard shortcuts are expressed with the name of a modifier key and another key that must be pressed at the same time, such as, "Press Command-S to save the file." However, the Command key has always been a source of confusion: the key often appears with a 🍎 or ⌘ symbol.

- When I refer to a "gesture," I'm talking about using finger motions on a laptop trackpad or Apple's Magic Trackpad. For example, the gesture to open the Mission Control interface is to swipe upward with three fingers.

- In a few places, I refer to more information found in the Mac Help files. Choose Mac Help from the Help menu.

1

Meet Mountain Lion

Apple is known for its outstanding industrial design, from the first eye-catching and colorful iMacs to the svelte MacBook Air. But here's the hiding-in-plain-sight secret about the Mac: No matter what computer you're on, you interact with its operating system, OS X. A Mac could just as easily be a large gray box under your desk and you'd still get the full Mac experience thanks to the software that runs the machine.

Mountain Lion incorporates concepts from the iPad, such as controlling some actions using finger gestures if you own a trackpad; accessing applications on one screen, called Launchpad; viewing notifications; automatic saving of documents; and working with applications full screen. In this chapter, I answer some basic questions about OS X for readers who may be new to the Mac (perhaps you own an iPad, iPhone, or iPod touch; or you're switching from a Windows PC) or just new to Mountain Lion.

The Pocket Guide Overview of OS X Mountain Lion

I've learned to never assume a person's level of computer experience. Some people have used only a few features to accomplish specific tasks, while other people dig deep into the machine's capabilities and settings. To get us on the same page, here are answers to common questions— feel free to skip ahead if this is familiar territory.

I've just bought a Mac. What exactly is Mountain Lion?

Mountain Lion is the latest version of OS X, the operating system that runs every modern Mac computer. Mountain Lion handles fundamental tasks like creating and organizing files and folders, and it includes applications for performing tasks such as sending and receiving email, listening to music, accessing the Web, organizing your schedule, backing up your data, and more. Technically, this version of the system is called OS X 10.8 Mountain Lion.

What is a user account and why am I creating one?

When you purchase a new Mac, part of the setup process involves creating your own specific identity within OS X, even if you're the only person who will use the computer. Creating a user account also involves assigning a password for security, which you use when installing new software or accessing some system preferences. Note that this account is not the same as the Apple ID that you may already use for iTunes or other Apple interactions. See Chapter 2 for more information about user accounts.

I don't have Mountain Lion yet, and I've heard that I can't buy it on disc. How do I upgrade my current Mac?

OS X has traditionally been distributed on CDs or DVDs, but starting with version 10.7 Lion, Apple chose to make OS X available only as a download from the Mac App Store. This means you need to make sure your Mac is running at least OS X 10.6.8 Snow Leopard or OS X 10.7 Lion and that you have access to sufficient Internet bandwidth to download an installer program that is about 4 GB (gigabytes).

Do I need a trackpad to use Mountain Lion?

Mountain Lion supports many kinds of gestures, so having some sort of tracking device—Apple's Magic Trackpad or Magic Mouse, or a laptop with a trackpad—is encouraged. But it's not required.

Will I be able to run all my old software in Mountain Lion?

No. Programs originally written for old Macs with PowerPC processors will no longer run at all, because Apple has removed Rosetta, the technology for translating PowerPC commands into ones an Intel processor can work with. If you rely on older software, it's time to look for alternatives or keep another Mac running Snow Leopard handy.

What is OS X Mountain Lion Server?

OS X Mountain Lion Server is an expanded version of OS X designed to act as a file or Web server, typically for businesses or small groups. With it, you can host your own email and calendar servers, for example, instead of relying on a company to provide those services. Mountain Lion Server is available from Apple for $19.99. I don't cover Mountain Lion Server in this Pocket Guide.

I'm new to the Mac, and the computer is on. Just what am I looking at?

Even if you've never used a Mac before, many of the interface elements are likely to be familiar. Here's a quick orientation to what you see (**Figure 1.1**).

Figure 1.1
The OS X interface

Menu bar ——

Finder window ——

Desktop ——

Dock ——

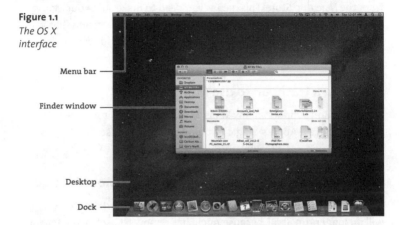

The menu bar

The menu bar runs along the top of the screen and provides commands, grouped into menus, for applications. You can always tell which program is currently active by looking for the name next to the Apple menu (🍎).

> **tip** The menu bar is translucent by default, so your desktop background image will show through it. If that's too distracting, go to the Desktop & Screen Saver preference pane, click the Desktop button, and deselect the Translucent Menu Bar option.

The icons on the right half of the menu bar show the status of various programs and processes, such as the strength of the Wi-Fi network and the current time.

The Finder and the Desktop

When you start up your Mac, the first thing you see is the Finder. It's the file navigation system that lets you manage the contents of your hard disk in floating windows and connect to other computers.

The Desktop is the background space behind your windows, where you can toss files and folders for easy access. But the Desktop is *also* a folder within your Home folder—in terms of structure, that's where the files live. So it's possible to see two copies of the same file in two different visual locations: on the background working area and within a window showing the contents of the Desktop folder.

I find that I typically ignore the visual space behind my windows (because it's often obscured by windows and applications) and open a new Finder window for the Desktop when I need something there. My wife, on the other hand, almost never opens the Desktop folder, because she knows, spatially, where a particular file appears on her workspace.

Windows

The significance of "windows" is nearly lost now, but back when all of our computer interaction involved nothing but lines of scrolling text, it was radical to show files within a floating rectangle. Resize and reposition windows as you see fit, and take advantage of the following window features in Mountain Lion (**Figure 1.2**).

Figure 1.2
Icons can be enormous in Mountain Lion.

- Window contents can be viewed as icons, as lists, in columns, and using Apple's Cover Flow mode (**Figure 1.3**). You may prefer one style, or you can mix and match them depending on what you're viewing.

Figure 1.3
The three other window views

List view

Column view

Cover Flow view

Using Icon or Cover Flow view works well when browsing a folder full of images so you can immediately see previews of the pictures, while List view is good for sorting files by name or by date.

tip When you're in Column view, you can drag a column divider to change the width of the column. If you hold Option while you do so, all of the columns resize equally.

tip It's easy to get lost in the Finder and not know where in the folder structure a particular file or folder is located. Choose View > Show Path Bar to display a selected item's hierarchy (Figure 1.4).

Figure 1.4
The Path Bar

Path Bar

- Drag the icon size slider in the lower-right corner of every window in Icon view to quickly enlarge or shrink the icons' sizes. (If you don't see this control, choose View > Show Status Bar.)

- Resize the window's dimensions by dragging any edge (instead of just the lower-right corner, as in previous versions of OS X). To resize the window from the center, hold the Option key as you drag. Or, hold Shift and drag to resize with the window's current aspect ratio.

- To configure how windows appear, including which columns appear, icon sizes, and text size, choose View > Show View Options.

tip You'll find plenty of other options for customizing the Finder's behavior by choosing Finder > Preferences. Determine which items appear in the sidebar and on the Desktop, give names to Finder labels, set which folder opens in every new window, and more.

The Toolbar

Occupying the top portion of every window, the Toolbar offers a pair of Back and Next buttons to navigate the folders you've viewed in that window; buttons for the window view styles; an Arrange menu for sorting window contents; a Share Sheet for sharing selected files; an Action menu that gives you a list of relevant actions based on what's selected; and a Spotlight search field.

Scroll bars

One interface departure in Mountain Lion—if you use a trackpad—is the seeming disappearance of scroll bars, the handles at the right edge of a window or sidebar that you drag to view more items. Don't worry, they're not gone: Position your mouse pointer over a window to make them appear (**Figure 1.5**). If you have a trackpad, drag with two fingers to scroll in any direction. (If a mouse is connected to the computer, the bars are always visible.)

Figure 1.5
Scroll bars visible

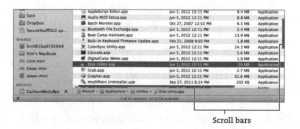

Scroll bars

tip Does scrolling seem *backward* to you? Apple reversed the scrolling direction in Lion to better replicate the way items scroll on the iPhone and iPad. So, to scroll to the bottom of a Web page in Safari, you swipe up, not down. If you want to go back to the old behavior, open the Trackpad preference pane, click the Scroll & Zoom button, and deselect the "Scroll direction: natural" setting. Or, if you have just a mouse, find the setting in the Mouse preference pane.

To make the scroll bars permanently visible, open System Preferences and change the scroll bars settings in the General preference pane.

The sidebar

The sidebar along the left side of a window contains shortcuts for many destinations, such as connected hard disks, available network volumes, common folders, and saved searches. Even better, you can add your own files, folders, or applications to the sidebar: just drag one to the sidebar and release the mouse button. (To remove an item, hold Command and drag it out of the sidebar.) This is a great location to put current project files or folders, because you can access the project's materials from any window. Or, choose View > Hide Sidebar to get it out of the way.

Be a Finder Neat Freak

Some people don't mind visual chaos, while others prefer everything to appear neat and orderly. Here are some tips for the latter.

- At any time in Icon view, choose View > Clean Up to align the icons to a grid.

- Choose View > Show View Options and adjust the Grid Spacing slider to move icons closer together or farther apart.

- In the View Options window, choose an option from the Arrange By pop-up menu to force icons to adhere to the grid.

- The View Options apply to the Desktop, too. Open the Desktop folder in a window, or just click the background, and bring up the View Options window to impose order on your workspace.

Helpful Window Shortcuts

Make your Finder explorations easier by using these shortcuts.

- Command-click a folder to open its contents in a new window.

- Option-click a folder to open its contents in a new window and close the previous window.

- Command-click a folder's name in the window's title to view a pop-up menu indicating its place in the disk hierarchy. You can then jump to a higher level by choosing it.

Get information about your system

If you ever need to find out something about your Mac, such as how much memory is installed or how much free hard disk space is available, choose About This Mac from the Apple menu (🍎) and then click the More Info button. The System Information application launches and provides you with a friendly glimpse of that information (**Figure 1.6**).

If you want to drill deeper into what's going on under the lid, click the System Report button that appears on the first screen.

Figure 1.6
About This Mac

2

Set Up Mountain Lion

Like Lion before it, Mountain Lion is available only as a download from the Mac App Store. This approach is convenient—you can upgrade in the middle of the night in your pajamas—but is also quite a change from the past, when you could insert a DVD and update from there.

Most of the information in this chapter is focused on upgrading from Lion or Snow Leopard (which are required for Mountain Lion). If instead you've bought a new Mac with Mountain Lion already installed, skip ahead to "Migrate Your Information" to learn how to get data from another Mac or from a Windows PC, and then to "Manage User Accounts" to learn important tips for working with your virtual identity within Mountain Lion. I also cover setting up a Boot Camp partition for running Microsoft Windows on your Mac (yes, you heard me correctly; it's a brave new world!).

Before You Upgrade

To ensure a smooth upgrade experience, and the safety of your existing data, take the following actions before upgrading to Mountain Lion.

- **Update your software.** Go to the Apple menu (), choose Software Update, and install any updates that appear. This step is particularly important if any firmware updates are available.

   If you're running a version of OS X prior to 10.6, you'll need to first purchase Snow Leopard and upgrade your Mac to it, since the Mac App Store requires version 10.6.

- **Turn off the original FileVault.** If you ever used FileVault under Snow Leopard or earlier, turn it off before upgrading. The original FileVault encrypted your Home directory, but the FileVault implementation in Lion and Mountain Lion is completely different—it encrypts the entire hard disk. Open the Security & Privacy preference pane, click the FileVault button, and then click the Turn Off FileVault button. You don't need to do this if you're using FileVault under Lion.

- **Back up your Mac.** *If you do nothing else, do this!* Should something go wrong during the upgrade process, you want to be able to quickly revert to your current version.

   If you're running Snow Leopard with a Time Machine backup, click the Time Machine icon () in the menu bar and choose Back Up Now. I also *highly* recommend making a duplicate of your hard disk; that's the quickest way to get back on your feet if something goes wrong. Jump ahead to "Make a Duplicate" in Chapter 9 for details.

- **Verify your hard disk to check for directory corruption issues.** Launch the Disk Utility application (find it in the Finder by choosing Go > Utilities) and click the Verify Disk button. If errors crop up, you'll need to restart the computer from the Recovery HD (Lion), your install disc

(Snow Leopard), or from another hard disk (like the duplicate you just made in the previous step) and run Disk Utility from there, because Disk Utility can't repair a disk that's currently running the computer.

- **Make sure you have sufficient bandwidth.** Mountain Lion is available only as an online download that weighs in at about 4.4 GB (gigabytes), so you'll need to be on a relatively fast Internet connection. That could be your home broadband, a coffeeshop with Wi-Fi, or your closest Apple retail store or authorized reseller.

Repairing the Startup Disk

Disk Utility can't repair a startup disk that's running the computer, just as you can't perform open-heart surgery on yourself (really, do not try that at home). Here's how to make repairs:

1. If you're running Lion, restart the Mac and hold the Command and R keys until the OS X Utilities window appears; skip to Step 4. For a Snow Leopard Mac, insert the disc, connect the hard disk, or plug in the other Mac.

2. Restart the computer, and hold the Option key; or, if you're starting from a second Mac, hold the T key to enter Target Disk Mode.

3. When the row of startup disks appears, choose the one you want.

4. Open Disk Utility: If you're starting from a CD, choose Disk Utility from the Utilities menu. If you've started up from another disk or Mac, choose Go > Utilities and open the application.

5. Select the computer's hard disk in the list at left, and then click the Repair Disk button. The repair could take several minutes.

6. Choose Quit from the Disk Utility menu and then restart the computer, using your internal hard disk as the startup volume.

Upgrade to Mountain Lion

After you've prepared your Mac for Mountain Lion, it's time to install the beast. Although Mountain Lion is distributed only online, the process will leave you purring.

1. Click the Mac App Store icon in the Dock to open it (**Figure 2.1**).

Figure 2.1
The Mac
App Store

2. Locate OS X Mountain Lion (it shouldn't be difficult, but if necessary use the Search field at the upper-right corner of the store window).

3. Click the price button ($19.99), and then click it again when the button reads "Buy App."

4. Enter your Apple ID (the same one you use for purchasing media from iTunes) and click the Buy button. The Mountain Lion installer appears in the Dock (under Snow Leopard) or in LaunchPad (Lion) and begins downloading.

5. Go grab a bite to eat, or go to bed, or do something else that occupies your time while the 4 GB installer downloads. To check its progress, click the Purchases button in the Mac App Store or view the progress bar on the icon in the Dock or in LaunchPad. You can continue to work on the computer while Mountain Lion downloads.

tip The Mac App Store puts the installer into the Applications folder. However, before running the installer, I recommend making a copy of it: In the Finder, choose Go > Applications (or press Command-Shift-A), and then drag the Mountain Lion installer to the Desktop while holding the Option key. Why? After the installation is finished, Mountain Lion deletes the installer. You can get it again if needed from the Mac App Store, but that involves another lengthy download. Having a copy is useful if you want to install Mountain Lion on another computer you own.

6. Click the Mountain Lion installer to launch it.

7. Click the Continue button on the opening screen, read the software license agreement, and agree to it by clicking the Agree button.

8. Click Install to put Mountain Lion on your Mac's internal hard disk (**Figure 2.2**). If other disks are attached to the Mac, click Show All Disks to choose another version of OS X to update, and then click the Install button.

Figure 2.2
Choose your startup disk.

9. Enter your administrator password and click OK to continue. The computer restarts as part of the process.

10. When the installation is finished, the computer restarts.

Make an Emergency Installation Disc

The biggest drawback to Apple's online-only distribution of Mountain Lion is that you don't have an installer on DVD that you can use to start up the computer for diagnostics. Mountain Lion does include the Recovery HD, a hidden partition that includes Disk Utility and a way to reinstall OS X (see Chapter 11), but that assumes your hard drive is functional. If your disk's hardware fails, that partition is gone, too. Although this procedure isn't blessed by Apple, here's a way to create a bootable installation disc on a DVD or a USB memory drive.

1. After downloading the Mountain Lion installer, locate it in the Applications folder; or, find the copy I suggested you make in the tip on the previous pages.

2. Right-click the application and choose Show Package Contents from the contextual menu.

3. Open the Contents folder and then the SharedSupport folder.

4. Double-click the InstallESD.dmg file to mount the disk image.

5. Launch Disk Utility from your Applications > Utilities folder.

6. Drag the mounted InstallESD disk image to the sidebar in Disk Utility if it's not already there.

6. To make a bootable DVD in Disk Utility, select the mounted InstallESD image and click the Burn button. Insert a blank DVD and follow the instructions.

   To make a bootable USB drive, make sure it's plugged into the computer, select the mounted InstallESD image, and click the Restore button at the top of the right column. Specify the USB drive in the Destination field. Lastly, click the Restore button.

The resulting disc or USB drive can be used to start up the Mac and give you access to the same tools found in the Recovery HD.

Installing onto a Clean Slate

What if you want to start over from scratch? You may want to erase your hard disk and then add your earlier data from a backup—perhaps to weed out any hidden gremlins. Start up from another drive (such as a duplicate, or the emergency disc I describe on the opposite page), use Disk Utility to wipe your hard disk, and then install Mountain Lion. Then, use Migration Assistant, described below, to bring your data over from your backup. If you take this route, make sure you first deauthorize iTunes and deactivate any software, such as the Adobe Creative Suite, that requires online authentication.

Migrate Your Information

If you've just purchased a Mac with Mountain Lion installed, the first thing you'll see is a series of questions that establish the country in which you live and the keyboard layout you'd like to use. The installer also asks if you'd like to migrate data from another Mac, a Windows PC, or a Time Machine backup or other disk. (You can also choose to skip this step and migrate later. If that's the case, jump ahead to "Manage User Accounts" later in this chapter, and then return here when you're ready to migrate.)

If you've already skipped past the introductory material, choose Go > Utilities in the Finder and launch the Migration Assistant. This nifty utility copies your documents, settings, Web bookmarks, and other information that would be annoying and time-consuming to copy manually. To transfer data between two computers, the machines must be on the same network—which could be as simple as stretching an Ethernet cable between them.

tip If you're migrating from one Mac to another, and both machines include a FireWire port or a Thunderbolt port, I recommend connecting them using Target Disk Mode, which makes the new Mac see the old one as if it's just another hard disk. String a FireWire or Thunderbolt cable between them and restart the Mac that you're migrating *from* (the source Mac). As the computer starts up, press and hold the T key until you see a large white FireWire or Thunderbolt logo on the screen. Then, in Migration Assistant, choose "From Time Machine or other disk" and specify the source hard disk.

Migrate from another Mac or from a Windows PC

Moving your data from an existing computer can make it seem as if you never left the old one.

1. At the screen asking if you want to migrate your information in the Mountain Lion installer, choose "From another Mac" or "From a Windows PC" and click Continue.

   Or, in the standalone Migration Assistant application, choose "From another Mac, PC, Time Machine backup, or other disk," click Continue, and then choose "From a Mac or PC" (**Figure 2.3**). Click Continue again.

Figure 2.3
*Migrate data
from another
computer on
the network.*

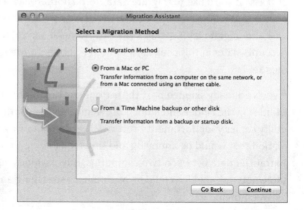

2. On the computer you're migrating from, launch Migration Assistant and choose the "To a Mac" method. Click Continue.

   (If you're migrating from a Windows PC, first download and install the Windows Migration Assistant on your PC from www.apple.com/migrate-to-mac/.)

3. Both computers then display a numeric passcode to verify that they're communicating correctly. If the passcodes match, click Continue on both machines. See "Perform the migration," below.

Migrate from a Time Machine backup or other disk

It may be easier to restore a Mac's data from a Time Machine backup or from a hard disk that contains another backup (such as a duplicate).

1. At the screen asking if you want to migrate your information in the Mountain Lion installer, choose "From Another disk." (In the Migration Assistant application, this option is labeled "From a Time Machine backup or other disk." Just so we're on the same page.) Click Continue.

2. Select the disk you want to use; if just one disk is attached when running the Mountain Lion installer, it's automatically selected.

3. Click Continue and proceed to the next section.

Perform the migration

Once a connection has been established, Migration Assistant provides a list of the data on the other Mac, with everything selected.

1. In the Select Items to Migrate screen, choose which items to exclude from the transfer (**Figure 2.4**, on the next page). For example, you may wish to migrate just one user account, or not include a user's large Music folder. Click the expansion triangles to reveal more detail; for users, that includes the contents of their Home folders.

Figure 2.4
Choose data to migrate.

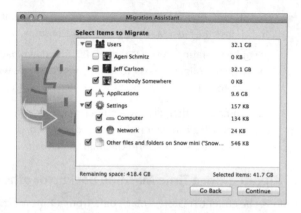

 When you click a user name to deselect it, the checkmark becomes a dash, indicating that some data will still be copied—even though none of the user's Home folder items are selected. What's going on? Selecting any user account copies system and preference files in the user's Library folder.

2. Click Continue to initiate the transfer. Depending on the amount of data chosen, the migration could take several minutes or more than an hour.

3. When the process is finished, quit Migration Assistant. If you're still in the Mountain Lion installer, click Continue.

tip Be sure to connect the power cord if you're migrating from a laptop, since the migration process can take quite a while.

note When you migrate information to a new machine during the first setup, the account on your old Mac becomes the main account on the new one. However, when you migrate using the Migration Assistant on a Mac that's already set up, your old Mac account is added as a separate account. (See "Manage User Accounts" on the next page.)

After completing the migration, you'll need to reactivate any software that uses per-machine licensing, reauthorize iTunes, and otherwise bring your status to the same point of your other Mac before you migrated. As you start working on the new system you may—how best to put this?—run into minor snags where settings may not have transferred correctly, or where software that works under Snow Leopard or Lion behaves erratically under Mountain Lion. Migration Assistant does a great job, but it doesn't always catch everything.

Manage User Accounts

When you interact with OS X, the operating system sees you as a *user account*. You may have just one account, or you may share a Mac and set up separate accounts for each member of your family. Although each account shares resources from the system—such as the applications and connection to the Internet—the accounts exist as separate identities, each with its own settings, documents, and other data (**Figure 2.5**).

Figure 2.5
User accounts are separate, but each uses the same system resources.

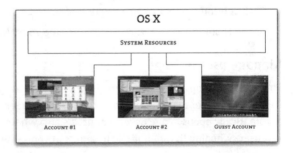

Set up the first user during installation

The first time you install OS X on a Mac, or the first time you start up a brand new Mac, you're asked to enter information to create a user account. (If you opted to migrate data from another computer, your previous account is used.)

1. Enable Location Services on the screen that appears. Location Services uses data such as the names of nearby Wi-Fi networks to determine your Mac's location for some features, such as Find My Mac.

2. Enter your Apple ID if you already have one, or click Skip. (You can also choose to set up an Apple ID here.)

3. After viewing Apple's legalese, click Continue. To create the first user account, type a user name and, optionally, a shortened version of that—the installer makes a suggestion based on the name you enter.

4. Enter a secure password (don't choose obvious things like a pet's name or your birthday, but do think of something that will be easy to remember; you'll need it often).

5. By default, the new account is set to require a password at login. To skip login, deselect the "Require password when logging in" checkbox.

6. Click Continue to create the account and set your time zone.

At the Thank You screen, click the Start Using Your Mac button.

Manage user settings

The Users & Groups preference pane is where you manage accounts and configure whether the computer presents a login screen at startup or automatically opens in one user account. It's also where you can enable fast user switching to run multiple accounts at the same time. To access the Users & Groups preference pane, do the following.

1. From the Apple menu ($\bullet$), choose System Preferences; or, click its icon in the Dock.

2. Click the Users & Groups icon (**Figure 2.6**) to open the pane.

Figure 2.6
The Users &
Groups icon
in System
Preferences

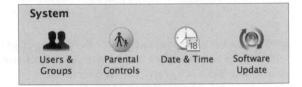

Password pane

The Password pane offers options for managing your password and
identity (**Figure 2.7**).

Figure 2.7
The Users &
Groups Password
pane

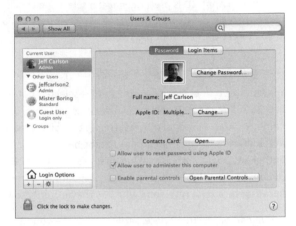

- Click the Change Password button to assign a new master password
  (see Chapter 10).

- Feel free to change your name in the Full Name field. This information
  is used at login and also when sharing files (see Chapter 8).

- Clicking the picture field brings up a menu with some stock icons, or you can choose Edit Picture to take a photo of yourself (if your Mac has a camera).

> **tip** You can also use Cut and Paste to change the picture. Copy an image from another source (such as a Web page), click the picture field to select it, and choose Edit > Paste. Use the controls that appear to specify the size of the image, and click the Set button to apply it.

- If you have an Apple ID (and you didn't provide it during installation), click the Set button to enter it and your password. If you don't have an Apple ID, click the Set button and then click the Create Apple ID button.

- When an Apple ID is present, you can select the checkbox for "Allow user to reset password using Apple ID." That provides a fallback in case you forget your account password.

Administrator and regular accounts

You'll notice that in Figure 2.7, one item is selected but grayed out: Allow user to administer this computer. User accounts come in two varieties: administrators and regular users. The first account created under OS X is automatically set up as an administrator, because you frequently need to authorize actions such as making changes to settings (like these account options). Parental controls are also disabled for an admin account, because the admin is the one who has the authority to set the controls.

Regular accounts aren't necessarily restricted—you can still install software and perform other common tasks—but they're not able to change parameters such as system preferences.

Manage login items

Some software packages install programs that need to run invisibly in the background (such as iTunesHelper), while others provide the option to launch at startup. The Login Items pane controls what components automatically run and lets you add others.

Add a login item

Any file—applications, movies, documents, whatever—can be set to launch at login. On my Mac, for example, I've included an application launcher (LaunchBar) and a password manager (Yojimbo) as login items so I don't have to remember to launch them individually.

1. Click the Add (+) button below the list (**Figure 2.8**).

Figure 2.8
The Login Items pane

2. Locate the item to add in the dialog that appears, and click Add.

    To make an item invisible after it has opened, select the Hide checkbox.

To remove an item, click the Delete (–) button. As you'll see in Chapter 11, deleting login items is helpful when trying to troubleshoot problems.

tip Does the Login Items list contain something that looks questionable? Control-click or right-click the item and choose Reveal in Finder to locate the file, which may provide a hint as to which software owns it.

Create a new user account

If multiple people share one Mac, it's a good idea to set up separate user accounts for each person. Their files and settings are stored in their own directories, and they can customize the desktop background, screen saver, and viewing preferences to their hearts' content.

1. In the Users & Groups preference pane, click the lock icon and enter your administrator password to access the controls you'll need.

2. Click the Add (+) button below the accounts list. A dialog appears (**Figure 2.9**).

Figure 2.9
Creating a new user account

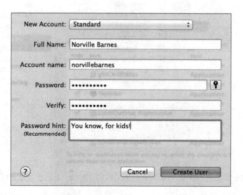

3. Choose the type of account to set up from the New Account pop-up menu. Standard is the default, but you can also make the account an

Administrator or a Managed with Parental Controls account (such as for a child's use).

The Sharing Only and Group options are used for sharing files with other computers; see Chapter 8.

4. Enter a name for the account in the Full Name field. A corresponding short version is created automatically in the Account Name field (all lowercase, with no spaces). Edit the account name here if you'd like—it's your only chance to change it.

> **tip** You can go back and edit an account's full name, but an account name cannot be changed once the account is set up.

5. Enter a password in the Password and Verify fields. (OS X can help you choose a good password using the key button to the right of the Password field; see Chapter 10 for more information.)

Also enter a password hint that will be displayed on the login screen if you enter the incorrect password three times.

6. Click the Create User button, after which your new account appears in the accounts list.

> **note** From a security standpoint, it's better to create a new standard (non-admin) account as your main user account, because it reduces the chance that malicious software could take over an administrator account. However, I've always run OS X as an admin user; gaining access to the deeper levels of the operating system still calls for an admin password whether you're logged in as an administrator or not. I'd rather do my best to stay away from obvious sources of malware (adult Web sites, suspicious downloads, and the like) than to juggle multiple user names and passwords during my everyday work. If you're concerned, by all means create and use a new non-admin account, but I've found it to be not worth the hassle.

tip After you've created a new standard account, you can turn it into an administrator account by selecting the "Allow user to administer this computer" option. Similarly, you can revoke admin status by deselecting that option in an admin account. However, at least one admin account must be present.

Create a "Bare" Account for Testing

Even if you're the only person using your Mac, you should create a new standard user account and leave it as unchanged as possible. If you run into a problem where programs are crashing or don't appear to be working correctly, the culprit could be one of your login items or software running invisibly in the background.

One of the first troubleshooting steps to take in such situations is to locate the problem. Restart the Mac and boot into the test user account, and see if the problem persists. If it doesn't, one of the login items in your regular account could be the cause.

Create a Guest User account

Perhaps this has happened to you. A houseguest asks to check her email using your computer, but in the process moves your Finder icons, edits your Web bookmarks, or maybe even deletes some files. The Guest User account avoids all that hassle, providing a bare-bones, temporary environment. When your houseguest is finished, all changes (including any files saved to the hard disk) are deleted.

The Guest User account is not enabled by default. Here's how to set it up.

1. In the Users & Groups preference pane, click the lock icon and enter your administrator password.

2. Click the Guest User item.

3. Select the option labeled "Allow guests to log in to this computer" (**Figure 2.10**).

Figure 2.10
Enable the Guest User.

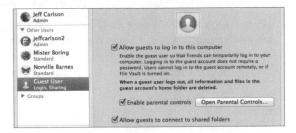

> **tip** You can apply parental controls to a Guest User account to limit how someone uses the computer. For example, you may want to restrict which applications are launched and set a time limit for use. Select the "Enable parental controls" checkbox, and then click the Open Parental Controls button.

Set login options

Click the Login Options button at the bottom of the accounts list to configure how the computer starts up (**Figure 2.11**).

Figure 2.11
The Login Options pane

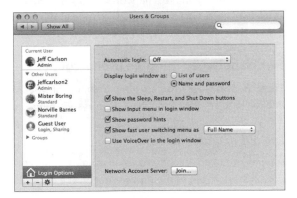

- Automatic login loads the user you specify; this is the normal behavior on a new OS X installation. Choose Off from the pop-up menu to display the login screen at startup or when you log out of an account.

- The login window can show a list of users or just empty fields for entering a name and password. Choose the latter if you want a little more security (since someone trying to log in to your computer would need to know both the account name and the password to gain access).

- Showing the Restart, Sleep, and Shut Down buttons provides shortcuts to these commands. When restarting or shutting down, you must still enter the name and password of any account that's currently logged in.

- Choose the "Show Input menu in login window" option to select from a pop-up list of other installed languages.

- If "Show password hints" is selected, the hint you provided when setting up a password appears after a wrong password is entered three times.

- See the next section for more on the fast user switching option.

- The option "Use VoiceOver in the login window" speaks the name of highlighted objects.

- If you're connecting to a network account server, click the Join button. (Network accounts are outside the scope of this book; see the built-in Mac Help about directory services for more details.)

Switch between multiple user accounts

There are two ways to access other accounts on your Mac: log out of one and log in to another, or enable fast user switching.

Log out of a user account

Logging out of an account closes all running applications and "shuts down" the user, but without powering off the computer.

1. Choose Apple () > Log Out *user's name*, or press Command-Shift-Q.

2. At the screen confirming that you want to quit all applications and log out, click the Log Out button. If any applications contain unsaved work, you're given the opportunity to save and close the documents before the programs quit.

To pick up where you left off next time, make sure the option "Reopen windows when logging back in" is selected. OS X will restore the environment as it was when you left it.

The login screen appears, giving you the option of logging in to another account.

Fast user switching

The problem with logging out of an account is that whatever you were working on is interrupted. A better approach is to enable fast user switching, located in the Login Options pane. This feature lets you run multiple users simultaneously.

When activated, a new menu item appears in the upper-right corner of the screen, which can display an icon (to save space) or the current user's full name or short name.

1. Click the fast user switching menu to reveal a list of accounts on the machine (**Figure 2.12**).

Figure 2.12
*The fast user
switching menu*

2. Select an account you wish to open. You can also choose to display just the login window (such as when you're going to be away from the computer and want to restrict access to it).

3. Enter the account's password and wait while it starts up.

 tip When you log in to another account using fast user switching, your current account effectively goes to sleep. It's not entirely dormant, though. Messages, for example, includes a preference to automatically set its status to Away, go offline, or remain open when you're in another account.

Delete an account

If a user account is no longer useful to you, it can be removed.

1. In the Users & Groups preference pane, click the lock icon and enter an administrator's name and password.

2. Click the Delete (–) button at the bottom of the accounts list.

3. In the dialog that appears, choose what is to be done with that user's data: save the Home folder in a disk image to be read later, leave the files in place, or delete the Home folder.

4. Click the Delete User button.

tip To delete the current active account, you'll need to log out and log back in as another user.

Run Windows Using Boot Camp

Praising the virtues of OS X compared to Microsoft Windows can be entertaining, but in reality, some people need to use Windows: their business requires Windows-only software, for example. A great but often overlooked feature of OS X is Boot Camp, a technology that enables you to install and run Windows on your Mac.

Mountain Lion does not include a copy of Windows, of course. Boot Camp is just a framework for installing Microsoft's operating system. But it's not running in emulation: Without Apple's distinctive hardware styling, you wouldn't know you were using a Mac.

Boot Camp makes significant changes to your hard disk structure, so make sure you have plenty of free space on the drive and that you've backed up your Mac. Apple's Boot Camp Assistant software provides extensive instructions on setting up Boot Camp, but here's an overview.

1. Launch Boot Camp Assistant, which is found in the Utilities folder within your Applications folder (or choose Go > Utilities in the Finder). Click the Print Installation & Setup Guide button to get the detailed instructions. Click Continue to proceed.

2. Download the Windows support software for your Mac by clicking Continue on the next screen. This software handles hardware-specific things like keyboard backlighting and trackpad control. After the software is downloaded, choose to save it to a blank CD or DVD or to an external drive (like a USB thumbdrive). Click Continue, specify the destination, and click Save to copy the files.

3. Choose a partition size: half of the volume (click the Divide Equally button) or a custom size (drag the divider between the partitions) (**Figure 2.13**, on the next page).

4. Click the Partition button to divide the disk. Your OS X data remains intact.

5. Insert the Windows installation disc and click the Start Installation button. The computer restarts from the Windows disc and runs the installer program.

Figure 2.13
*Split your hard
disk into two
partitions.*

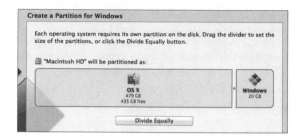

Switch between OS X and Windows

Boot Camp does not allow you to run both OS X and Windows at the
same time. Instead, you must choose which environment to start up in.
The Startup Disk preference pane can set your preference, but here's an
easier way:

1. Restart your machine and hold the Option key as it boots up.

2. Select the partition you want to use as the startup disk, then press
   Return or Enter.

   The next time you restart your computer, the Mac honors the setting
   in the Startup Disk preference pane, regardless of which partition you
   previously booted into.

> **tip** Although Boot Camp does not allow it, programs such as VMware
> Fusion (www.vmware.com) and Parallels Desktop (www.parallels.com)
> do let you run OS X and Windows simultaneously. In fact, they can both use
> your Boot Camp partition as the Windows environment without having to log
> out of OS X.

> **tip** Boot Camp under Mountain Lion installs disk drivers that allow you to
> access your Mac volumes from within Windows Explorer. Previously, a
> Windows Boot Camp installation wouldn't recognize the Mac-formatted
> volumes on the same hard disk.

3

Apps, the Dock, and Mission Control

Whenever you're *doing* something in OS X, you're doing it in an application. Writing in Microsoft Word or BBEdit; correcting photos in iPhoto or Adobe Photoshop; crunching numbers in Numbers; editing video in iMovie...you're using features included in an application.

This chapter covers how to run applications, as well as how to install and update them—a more complicated topic than one might expect, but made easier via the Mac App Store. And we can't talk about applications without looking at the Dock, Apple's go-to place for accessing applications (and more), and switching between apps using Mission Control.

Launch Applications

Starting an application is known as *launching*, no doubt because in the early days of computers, "launching" sounded more exciting than "wait several minutes while the machine copies data to its memory." Technology has advanced, thank goodness, so now most applications start up in a few seconds. Two methods of launching are available, depending on what you're more comfortable with: using Launchpad, or opening in the Finder.

Use Launchpad

Launchpad is a way to launch applications without digging into your Applications folder or junking up your Dock. Like the home screen on iOS devices, Launchpad displays large icons of every program onscreen. To use Launchpad, do the following:

1. Click the Launchpad icon in the Dock, or, on a trackpad, pinch inward with four fingers. The Launchpad interface takes over the screen (**Figure 3.1**).

Figure 3.1
Find and launch applications using Launchpad.

Launchpad icon   Launchpad navigation

 tip   If you use more than one monitor, Launchpad appears on whichever screen contains the Dock.

2. To switch among the Launchpad screens and view more applications, click anywhere on the screen and drag left or right; press the left or right arrow key on your keyboard; swipe with two fingers; or click a navigation circle.

tip Mountain Lion delivers a great improvement to Launchpad: Start typing the name of an app you want to launch. The word appears in the Search field at the top of the screen, and only apps matching the text appear.

3. Click or tap an icon to launch that application.

To exit Launchpad, click once on a space not occupied by an icon, press the Esc key, or pinch outward with four fingers.

Organize applications in Launchpad

One problem with Launchpad is that all your applications appear there, including ones you seldom or never use (such as program uninstallers or special-use utilities). To make Launchpad more useful, consider rearranging the icons or grouping them into folders.

To move an icon to a new location, click and drag it where you want; other icons shift out of the way to free up space. If you want to move an icon to a different Launchpad screen, drag the application to the edge of the screen until the previous or next set of icons appears.

To group applications into folders, do the following:

1. Drag an application icon onto the top of another icon (**Figure 3.2**).

Figure 3.2
I've dragged one icon onto another to create this new folder.

The two icons are enclosed in a folder (which looks like a square container, but Apple calls it a folder) and then appear in a row below the folder icon.

2. OS X suggests a name for the group based on the type of applications in it. To rename it, click once to select it and then type a new name.

3. To add more applications, click outside the folder to close it and then drag other programs onto the folder's icon.

Grouping applications into folders doesn't actually create new folders on your hard disk—the organization is used solely by Launchpad.

Remove an application from Launchpad

Any application you've purchased from the Mac App Store can be easily deleted from within Launchpad. (You can't remove applications included with OS X or ones installed by other means.) When you delete an app, it's gone immediately—it's not even moved to the Trash. However, you can re-download it from the Mac App Store later for free if needed.

1. Hold the Option key until the icons begin to shake. (You can also click and hold an application to make them shake.)

2. Click the X button at the upper-left corner of the icon.

3. In the dialog that appears, click the Delete button (**Figure 3.3**).

4. Click an empty area to exit the mode, or press Esc. If you held the Option key in step 1, you can ignore this step.

Figure 3.3
*Delete an app
from Launchpad.*

Use the Finder

Use any of the following methods to launch applications.

- Select an application and double-click its icon. Programs are stored in the Applications folder (choose Go > Applications, select the Applications item in a window's sidebar, or click the Applications folder in the Dock).

- If an application resides in the Dock, click its icon there (see "Use the Dock," later in this chapter).

- Click the Spotlight icon in the menu bar (or press Command-space) and start typing an application's name (**Figure 3.4**). Click it to launch.

Figure 3.4
Find and launch applications using Spotlight.

- In the Finder, double-click a file to open it; the application associated with that file launches if it's not already running.

- With an application or file selected, press Command-down arrow or choose File > Open (Command-O).

Open files using a different application

When you double-click a file in the Finder, which application will open it? The answer depends on the filename extension. Some formats are specific to one application; others, such as those ending in .pdf or .doc, can be read by many programs.

- Drag a document onto an application's icon to open it in that program.

- Select the file and choose File > Open With, and then choose an application. (If the program you have in mind isn't listed, click Other and locate it.) The Open With option appears on the contextual menu, too (Control-click or right-click a file to view the menu).

Change a file's default application

If you double-click a file and an unintended application launches, do the following to change which program is assigned to that file type.

1. Select a file in the Finder and choose File > Get Info (Command-I) to bring up the Get Info dialog.

2. Under Open With, choose an application from the pop-up menu to use for opening that file (**Figure 3.5**). If the program you have in mind isn't listed, click Other and locate it.

Figure 3.5
Choose an application to open the file.

3. To associate all files of that type with one application, click the Change All button in that pane.

4. In the dialog that appears, click Continue to apply the change.

tip I've used LaunchBar (www.obdev.at/products/launchbar) for opening applications (and doing much more) since before Apple introduced Spotlight. I find it to be more responsive and highly recommend it.

Use the Dock

The Dock, that three-dimensional row of icons that runs along the bottom of the screen, performs several duties. Primarily it's an application launcher, but it can also show you at a glance which programs are currently running. Its contents aren't limited to applications, either: Store documents and folders there to access them quickly without digging through the Finder to locate them.

Open applications from the Dock

The names of items in the Dock appear when you move the pointer over them (**Figure 3.6**). To open an application from the Dock, just click its icon.

Figure 3.6
Click an application's icon on the Dock to open it.

A program doesn't need to be in the Dock before it can be opened. Once any application is launched, its icon appears. When you quit the program, its icon is removed.

Choose which applications appear in the Dock

Apple loads its favorite applications into the Dock when Mountain Lion is installed, but you can add, remove, and rearrange icons to suit your preferences.

Add an item

Drag an application (or any other item) from the Finder to the Dock. Other icons politely move out of the way to welcome the newcomer.

note When you add something to the Dock, you're actually adding an *alias* that points to the original. The actual file remains in place within the folder hierarchy.

Another way to add an item permanently is to move it to a new position in the Dock. Drag the icon of a running application elsewhere in the Dock; OS X assumes that if you're going to enough trouble to specify where you want the program to appear, you want it to stay put.

Remove an item

To remove an application, drag its icon from the Dock; it disappears in a puff of smoke. Alternatively, Control-click (or right-click) the icon and choose Options > Remove from Dock (**Figure 3.7**). (The Finder and Trash, and any running applications, cannot be removed.)

Figure 3.7
Control-click an application to reveal options.

Access folder contents using Stacks

The Dock is dominated by applications, but you can put anything into it for easy access. Drag a file or folder onto the right edge, just beyond the divider (**Figure 3.8**). One helpful trick is to move the folder containing an active project's files to the Dock.

Figure 3.8
Dragging a folder to the Dock

 For fast access to your programs, drag the Applications folder to the Dock.

To make it easier to reach the files in a folder, Apple created Stacks. Click a folder in the Dock to view its contents (**Figure 3.9**).

Figure 3.9
The Stacks fan view

Control how Stacks appear

Control-click or right-click a folder in the Dock to bring up a menu of options, including how the contents are sorted; whether the icon appears in the Dock as a single folder or a layered stack of files; and how to display the content when the folder is clicked:

- **Fan.** After clicking the folder in the Dock, click any file or folder in the fan to open it; files open in their associated applications, while folders open in new Finder windows. You can also click Open in Finder to view the contents of the folder in a window.

- **Grid.** Folders with many items appear in a grid. Unlike the fan display, if you click a folder here, its content appears within the grid. If there are more items than will fit in the window, a scrollbar appears at right. Click the back button to return to the enclosing folder's contents (**Figure 3.10**).

Figure 3.10
Viewing a subfolder in the grid view

Back button

tip With a folder open in grid view, press an arrow key to highlight the first item. Then, use the arrow keys to select the item you want, and press Return to open it. Or, press Esc to dismiss the window.

- **List.** The contents appear as list items. Highlighting a folder name displays another connected list of items.

- **Automatic.** OS X chooses whether to display the contents as a fan or a grid (but not a list), depending on the number of items.

tip Unfortunately, Stacks prevents the one action you would expect from clicking a folder in the Dock: simply opening the folder in a new window (which was the normal behavior before Stacks arrived in Leopard). To do this, Control-click or right-click the folder and choose Open "*folder name*" from the pop-up menu.

Customize the Dock

One of the first things I did with the Dock was move it to the right edge of my screen—I find it gets in the way at the bottom. A number of options are available for customizing the placement and appearance of the Dock. You can find these controls in three locations: choose Apple > Dock; open the Dock preference pane; or Control-click the divider between applications and documents.

- **Turn Hiding On.** With hiding enabled, the Dock slides off the screen when not in use. Move your pointer to the Dock area to make it reappear.

- **Turn Magnification On.** As you move the pointer over Dock items, they grow so you can see them better (**Figure 3.11**). With this feature enabled, control the amount of magnification in the Dock preference pane using the Magnification slider.

Figure 3.11
Dock magnification

Magnification can be helpful when you have many icons, because the Dock automatically shrinks to accommodate them all. However, I find it more annoying than useful.

- **Position on Screen.** Choose Left, Bottom, or Right. Positioning on the edges gives the Dock a different, simplified appearance (since the three-dimensional shelf doesn't make sense along the side).

- **Resize the Dock.** Click and hold the divider in the Dock and drag up or down to make the entire Dock larger or smaller.

Minimize windows to the Dock

The Dock is also a temporary holding pen for active windows. When you click any window's Minimize button (the yellow one at the top left corner), the window is squeezed into a space in the Dock. You can also double-click a window's title bar to minimize it, or choose Window > Minimize (Command-M) in many (but not all) applications.

To retrieve the minimized window, click its icon in the Dock.

Minimize into application icon

If you tend to store lots of documents in the Dock, here's a setting that promises to remove clutter. In the Dock preference pane, select the option labeled "Minimize windows into application icon." A window remains open but doesn't appear on the Dock. To make it visible again, Control-click or right-click the application icon and choose the window name from the pop-up list that appears.

tip Hold Shift when you click the Minimize button to watch the window's animation in slow motion. This feature was used in the first demos of OS X to show the power of the operating system's graphics capabilities, and apparently it was never removed. Why do it now? Because you can!

Dock Shortcut Commands

The following shortcuts make working with Dock items faster.

- Command-click any Dock icon to reveal the original item in the Finder.

- Option-click an application's Dock icon to hide all of its windows.

- Control-click or right-click an item to reveal a contextual menu containing more options, including a list of a document's open windows.

Switch Between Applications

OS X can juggle more than one running application at a time, but can you? Here are ways to switch between active programs.

- Click an icon in the Dock to bring it forward.

- Click an open document window to bring its application to the front.

- Press Command-Tab to display running applications as a row of large icons in the middle of the screen. Continue pressing the Tab key until the application you want is highlighted, then release the keys to bring that application to the front.

  You can also keep the keys pressed to cycle through the icons. Or, after you press Command-Tab, move the pointer to select the program you want. Or (yes, there's one more), press the left and right arrow keys while the icons are visible.

tip With the onscreen switcher visible and the Command key still pressed, highlight an icon and press Q to quit or H to hide (or show if already hidden) that application.

Show and hide applications

As you open more applications, their windows overlap one another, leading to a visual mess. Any application can be hidden from view when you're not using it. From the application menu, choose Hide *application name*, or press Command-H. You can also choose the Hide command located on the contextual menu that appears when you Control-click an icon in the Dock.

The program continues to run in the background—it's just out of the way. You can quickly see if a program is running by looking for the white dot beside its icon in the Dock.

note When you switch applications using the Dock or Command-Tab, all windows of that application come forward (except those that are minimized, of course).

Closing Documents vs. Quitting an Application

Here's something I see all the time. A person is finished with a document—let's say it's a Microsoft Word document—and so they click the red Close button in the upper-left corner of the document window. They then switch to another program and assume they quit Word. The problem is, Word is still running in the background; some programs consume a fair amount of system resources even when not active, which reduces performance in other applications.

Apple doesn't make this situation easier, as some of its software (like iMovie) quits when you close its one application window. Getting around this interface confusion is simple: be sure to quit an application when you're done with it. If you need it again, it will launch faster than the first time because OS X keeps some vital information for starting up programs in its cache on disk.

View Notifications

I don't need to be hyperconnected to what's going on at all times, but I also don't like to be in the dark. Mountain Lion's notifications pop up to alert you of important information such as new email and text messages, calendar events, reminders, and other timely snippets. Notifications appear at the top of the screen where you can see them (but won't block what you're currently doing) (**Figure 3.12**).

Figure 3.12
Notification from the Reminders application

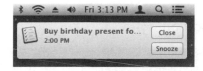

If you miss something that appeared, the new Notification Center collects those items in a single location; click the Notification Center button in the top-right corner of the screen to reveal it (**Figure 3.13**).

Figure 3.13
Notification Center

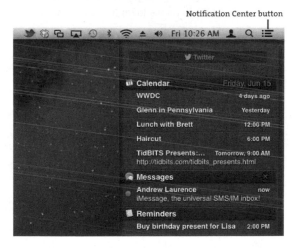

Double-click any item to jump to it in its parent application, such as an event in Calendar or a text in Messages. Clicking the X button to the right of an application name removes those items from the center, in case you want to de-clutter the list.

tip Are alerts and banners too distracting while you work? Turn them off: Drag the Notification Center down to reveal the Show Alerts and Banners option, and switch it to Off. Notifications continue to accumulate in the center until you're ready to view them.

Choose notification styles

Notifications appear as either banners, which display for a few seconds and then disappear, or alerts, which stay on the screen until you close or snooze (temporarily hide, like an alarm clock) them. In the Notifications preference pane, choose the style or even choose to prevent notifications from appearing for any application that supports notifications (**Figure 3.14**). To prevent notifications from appearing in the Notification Center entirely, drag the application's name down to the Not in Notification Center list at the bottom of the column.

Figure 3.14
Notifications preferences

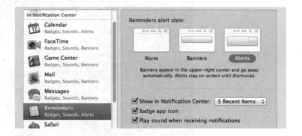

Share social updates from the Notification Center

Twitter and Facebook support (the latter scheduled for Fall 2012) is built into OS X, offering the ability to post status updates to those services without requiring a visit to their Web sites or the use of a third-party app. For example, click the Twitter button at the top of the Notification Center, enter your message in the field that appears, and click Send.

Use Mission Control

Apple has clearly spent a lot of time figuring out how to deal with visual overload as you work. Mission Control provides an overview of your running applications and their visible windows. (If you're coming to Mountain Lion from Snow Leopard, you'll notice Mission Control as a unified version of Spaces and Exposé.)

Activate Mission Control

Press Control-up arrow, press F3, or swipe up with three fingers to activate Mission Control. All your visible documents appear, grouped by application, along with the Dock (**Figure 3.15**).

Figure 3.15
Mission Control

If you want a better look at a document, especially if it's covered by another document, move your mouse pointer over its window until a blue highlight appears around the border (**Figure 3.16**). Then, tap the spacebar to perform a larger Quick Look view. Otherwise, click a window to exit Mission Control and bring it to the front of the rest.

Figure 3.16
Hover over a window to highlight it for a Quick Look view.

tip Mission Control is actually its own application in OS X and appears in the Dock and Launchpad for new user accounts. If you upgraded to Mountain Lion and would prefer to click an icon instead of press a function key or swipe a trackpad, go to the Applications folder and drag Mission Control to the Dock.

Configure Mission Control keyboard and mouse shortcuts

Everyone has their favored method of working, and the Mission Control preference pane enables you to configure shortcuts for activating Mission Control.

1. Open the Mission Control preference pane.

2. In the Keyboard and Mouse Shortcuts area, click the pop-up menus
    and choose the shortcuts you want to use. You can also hold the Shift,
    Command, Control, or Option keys to customize a shortcut; for exam-
    ple, to avoid conflicts with an application that might use a similar
    shortcut, you could set the Mission Control shortcut as Shift-F9.

 **Another option is to disable any of the shortcuts by choosing "–" from
the pop-up menu.**

**It's a good thing NASA didn't employ this Mission Control. If any appli-
cations are hidden, they don't appear in the overview screen. Also, any
documents that you've minimized to the Dock also appear missing. Fortunately,
the Dock is still visible, so you can click them there; but if you opted to minimize
windows into their application icons (as described a few pages back), the windows
are effectively invisible to Mission Control.**

Mission Control on Recent Macs

Current MacBook Pro models and Apple keyboards differ from earlier versions in how the function keys are laid out. Older Macs used
F9, F10, and F11 for different Exposé modes, but F3 (which is adorned
with a Mission Control icon) is now the preferred shortcut. That one
key offers all three modes:

■ Press the F3 key by itself to reveal all visible windows.

■ Press Control-F3 to view all windows from just the frontmost
application.

■ Press Command-F3 to push all windows offscreen.

■ Press Option-F3 to open the Mission Control preference pane.

Expand Your Desktop with Spaces

Do you ever wish you could have a wall of displays to hold all the windows and applications you're running? I've long advocated working with more than one monitor (I have an external display connected to my MacBook Pro), but even that seems limited some days. In Mountain Lion, you can create several virtual environments, called *spaces*, and switch between them, just as if you were looking at separate computer screens.

Switch between spaces

Initially, Mountain Lion offers two spaces: the desktop you're viewing and the Dashboard interface (I cover Dashboard later in this chapter). As more spaces are created, they're virtually positioned next to each other from left to right.

To switch between the spaces, do one of the following:

- Swipe left or right using three fingers.

- Press Control and the left or right arrow key.

- Press Control and the number key for the desktop space you want (more on desktops in a moment).

- Activate Mission Control and choose a space from the top of the screen (**Figure 3.17**).

Figure 3.17
Spaces appear at the top of the Mission Control screen.

tip **Normally, the Mission Control preference pane has the option "When switching to an application, switch to a space with open windows for** the application" selected. I find that setting to be too restrictive. Turn it off if you want to use windows from one application, such as Safari, in multiple spaces.

Run applications full screen

When you switch an application to full-screen mode, OS X treats it as its own space. Click the Full Screen () button in the upper-right corner of the application window to enter full-screen mode. Switch to the app by using any of the techniques on the previous page; in Mission Control, the app appears as a new space (**Figure 3.18**).

Figure 3.18
Mail is running full screen and in its own space.

For programs like Safari, which can have several windows (unlike Mail or iPhoto, which run in one window), each window can be expanded full screen as its own space.

To exit full-screen mode, position the mouse pointer at the top of the screen until the menu appears and then click the Full Screen button (**Figure 3.19**).

Figure 3.19
Exiting full-screen mode

note   Running apps full screen using multiple monitors is limiting, as the program appears only on your main screen. I would love to see the capability to use my second monitor to show the next space in line.

Create new desktops

The other way to take advantage of spaces is to create new desktops (up to 16). To create a new desktop, do the following:

1. Activate Mission Control.

2. Position your mouse pointer at the upper-right corner of the screen until you see a new Add (+) button (**Figure 3.20**). You can also press the Option key to make the button appear.

Figure 3.20
*Click to create
a new desktop
space.*

Add button

Mail

3. Click the Add button to create a new desktop.

> **tip** Each desktop can have its own background image. Go to the desktop you want, bring up the Desktop & Screen Saver preference pane, and choose a desktop image.

Delete a desktop

To remove a desktop, enter Mission Control and either hold the mouse pointer over the desktop icon for a few seconds or press the Option key. Then, click the X button that appears in the corner. Windows or applications in that desktop shift to another one.

Assign windows and applications to spaces

Mission Control is intended to reduce the clutter that comes with sharing everything on one screen, but you can also use the spaces aspect of the feature to separate workspaces. Perhaps you want to keep all of your social media applications in one space—Messages, Twitter, and Skype, for example—and then switch to another space where you can work on documents—Pages, OmniOutliner, or similar—without being visually interrupted when new messages arrive.

You can also set applications—such as Safari—so they appear in every space; restrict all windows from a specific app to one space; or assign windows to stay put in specific spaces. It can get pretty complicated, so here are the rules that govern how to control which items appear in which spaces.

Make an application appear in every space

I check Twitter many times during an average workday, so I like having a client tucked off to the side of my screen. To make an application appear in every space, right-click the app in the Dock, choose Options, and then choose All Desktops under the Assign To options (**Figure 3.21**).

Figure 3.21
Choose a desktop assignment for an application.

Assign an application to a specific space

Similarly, if you want all windows belonging to an application to remain in one space, navigate to the desktop you want, right-click the app in the Dock, and choose This Desktop from the Options submenu.

tip The Assign To options appear only when more than one space exists. If you don't see them, activate Mission Control and create a new desktop.

Place windows in a space

More helpful to me is the capability to use a desktop for a particular project. When writing and editing *TidBITS*, I primarily use BBEdit to work on text and Safari to look up information and manage our publishing system. But I also use BBEdit and Safari for other tasks in other spaces. So, I've reserved a desktop just for that purpose. Here's how to do it.

1. Create a new desktop or switch to the one you want to use.

2. Right-click an application (such as Safari) in the Dock and make sure the Assign To option is set to None.

3. Create a new document window; it remains anchored to that desktop.

You can also take an existing window from one desktop and move it to another by doing one of the following:

- Activate Mission Control and drag the window to the intended desktop (**Figure 3.22**).

Figure 3.22
Moving a BBEdit document to a desktop

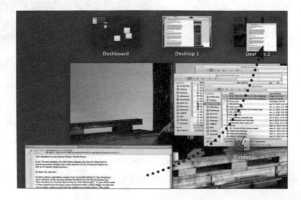

- Drag the window to the left or right edge of the screen and hold it there for a second until OS X switches to the next desktop.

- Click and hold the title bar of the window you want to move, and then press Control and an arrow key or number key representing the desktop to which you want to send the window.

Customize space behavior

Three settings in the Mission Control preference pane can dramatically affect how spaces behave.

- **Automatically rearrange spaces based on most recent use.** This option is useful if you primarily switch between spaces by first activating Mission Control. When you use a space, it slides to the left in the row's order, making it easily accessible. The problem with this approach is that you lose the previous order of spaces, making it easy to get lost if you primarily switch between spaces using gestures or keystrokes.

- **When switching to an application, switch to a space with open windows for the application.** When this option is selected, activating an application by clicking its icon in the Dock or choosing it via the application switcher jumps to the first space in which one of the application's documents appears.

- **Group windows by application.** This option layers all windows belonging to an application in a stack, as in Figure 3.22. Turn it off, and each window appears unobstructed on the screen.

View or hide applications using Exposé

Mission Control also incorporates Exposé, a feature with two other methods of reducing screen clutter: viewing application windows alone, and hiding everything to expose the Desktop beneath.

Application windows

Press F10 or Control-F3 to view all windows from just the frontmost application and temporarily hide other apps. To switch between applications without leaving Exposé, press Tab; or, press Command-Tab and choose an item from the application switcher (**Figure 3.23**).

Figure 3.23
Exposé showing application windows

Open windows —

Minimized or recently opened windows

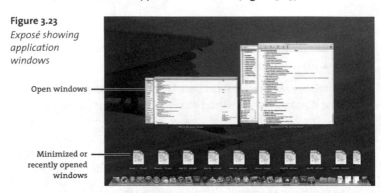

When an app has several documents open, even if they're located in different desktops, all of the windows appear. And, in an area at the bottom of the screen, you can access documents that are minimized to the Dock or have been recently opened. If more documents are available than will fit on the row, click the icons to the right or left to view more.

Show Desktop

Press F11 or Command-F3 to push everything aside temporarily, revealing the Desktop.

Use Exposé to move content between applications

Exposé can act as a shortcut when copying and pasting information between applications.

Move files in the Finder

Instead of spending time getting Finder windows aligned so you can move or copy a file from one to another, shuttle it through Exposé.

1. Using a mouse or trackpad, select a file you want to transport and move it slightly to tell the Finder it's in motion.

2. Press F10 or Control-F3 to engage Exposé. Alternatively, drag the file onto the Finder icon in the Dock and wait a moment for Exposé to activate.

3. Drag the file to your intended destination window and hold it there for a second until the highlight around the window flashes. Exposé kicks you back into the Finder with that window frontmost.

4. Release the mouse button. The file is moved or copied.

Move other data

The steps above apply to just about any other data you can move between applications. For example, suppose you want to include a portion of an article on the Web (including images or other formatting) in an outgoing email message.

1. In Mail, create a new outgoing message.

2. Select the content in Safari, then drag it slightly to "grab" it, and keep the mouse button held.

3. Press F10 or Control-F3 to engage Exposé.

4. Press Tab to switch the frontmost application until Mail appears; Exposé arranges Mail and your outgoing message in a grid.

5. Position the pointer over the message window and hold it there for a few seconds (**Figure 3.24**). The message comes to the front.

6. Release the mouse button to add the content.

Figure 3.24
Adding rich data to an outgoing Mail message via Exposé

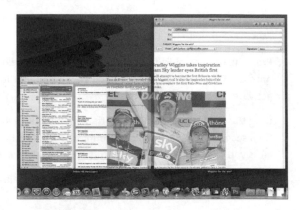

Dashboard

When you need just a snippet of information, Dashboard puts handy utilities, called *widgets*, on your screen when you need them. To activate Dashboard, press the F12 key, swipe left-to-right with three fingers, or choose Dashboard from within Mission Control (**Figure 3.25**).

Figure 3.25
Dashboard

tip In Mountain Lion, Dashboard appears as a separate space, but you can choose to make the widgets appear in a surface layer above your work instead. Open the Mission Control preference pane and deselect the option labeled "Show Dashboard as a space."

Configure a widget

When you move your pointer over a widget, look for a small "i" button. Click it to access the widget's settings (**Figure 3.26**).

Figure 3.26
Edit a widget's settings.

Configure widget

Add or remove widgets

Dashboard appears with four widgets by default, but more are available.

1. With Dashboard active, click the plus (+) button in the lower-left corner of the screen. That reveals a screenfull of widgets.

2. Click a widget to add it to the dashboard. You can include more than one copy of a widget; for example, add multiple Weather widgets to track different cities.

To remove a widget, click the close box that appears in the upper-left corner when the additional widgets are visible.

tip A faster way to remove a widget is to move your pointer over it and hold the Option key. Click the close box that appears.

Install Applications

When the time comes to install other applications on your Mac, several options await. Even now, decades into personal computing, installing software can be confusing. Here are the common methods of doing it.

Buy from the Mac App Store

Take a look at your Desktop or Downloads folder. Do you see any disk image files left over from when you needed to upgrade some software or install something new? Perhaps the image itself is still mounted. The Mac App Store is one of my favorite OS X features because it brings simplicity to a task that for too long has been complicated and unfriendly to inexperienced computer users. Installing software shouldn't be so hard, and now it doesn't have to be.

You're already familiar with this process, since Apple distributed Mountain Lion exclusively through the Mac App Store. But for reference, here are the basics of buying and installing an app.

1. Open the Mac App Store application by clicking its icon in the Dock.

2. Locate an app you wish to purchase.

3. Click the price button, which becomes a Buy App button (**Figure 3.27**).

Figure 3.27
Buying an app

4. Click the Buy App button and enter your Apple ID and password. The app downloads and appears in Launchpad (**Figure 3.28**).

Figure 3.28
The application installing within Launchpad

tip   One of my favorite features of the Mac App Store is the ability to easily install software you've already purchased onto any computer you own. When you log in using your Apple ID, the Mac App Store knows which programs you've purchased; click the Install button to download and install one without fuss.

Download from the Internet

Thanks to online distribution, you often don't need to bother with discs (and the bloated packaging around most of them).

1. Download the software from a company's Web site. It will be packaged as an archive (with a .zip or .hqx filename extension) or as a disk image (ending in .dmg).

2. Locate the downloaded file. In Safari, you can click the Show in Finder button (the magnifying glass icon) next to the file's name in the Downloads window (**Figure 3.29**).

Figure 3.29
Locating the installer you just downloaded

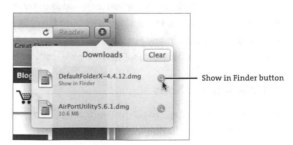

Show in Finder button

You can also open the Downloads folder in your Home folder; OS X puts that folder in the Dock by default.

3. Double-click the file to open it. If it's a disk image, a virtual volume appears on the Desktop and, usually, a new window appears with the volume's contents (**Figure 3.30**).

Figure 3.30
A mounted disk image

Mounted disk image

> **tip** Double-clicking the file in the Downloads folder also opens the disk image and saves a step. However, I'm taking the longer route here to explain where the important pieces reside.

Install from a disc

If you purchase a physical copy of a program, it most likely is stored on an installer disc. Insert the disc into your Mac's optical drive and read the next section. If you own a Mac that has no optical drive, you can access the disc from another computer on your network that does: Insert the disc into that machine's optical drive, and then, on your Mac, click the Remote Disc item in any Finder window's sidebar. Select the other computer and open the disc as if it were physically attached to the Mac.

Installation methods

With a disc or disk image mounted on the Desktop, you'll encounter one of the following installation methods.

- **Drag and drop.** Simply drag the software's icon to your Applications folder. The developer may have included an alias to the folder in the disk image, in which case you can just drag to that (**Figure 3.31**).

Figure 3.31
Drag-and-drop installation

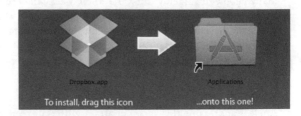

Dropbox.app

Applications

To install, drag this icon   ...onto this one!

- **Run an installer program.** Double-click the software's installer program, which should be clearly marked. You'll need to provide your administrator password to grant the program access to write its files, and most likely read and agree to a terms of service contract. Follow the installer's instructions.

Automatically install on other Macs

If you use more than one Mac, a clever setting will install an application on all your machines after you purchase it on one. Go to the Software Update preference pane and click the option labeled Automatically download apps purchased on other Macs.

After the installation

When the program has been copied or the installer is finished, don't forget to eject the physical disc or mounted disk image: Select it on the Desktop and choose File > Eject (Command-E); click the Eject button in the menu bar; or click the Eject button to the right of the item's name in a window's sidebar. At this point you can also delete the original file stored in the Downloads folder.

Stay Safe with Gatekeeper

Many people mistakenly think that their Macs can become infected by malicious software ("malware") from picking up a virus somewhere on their Internet travels. In reality, viruses are practically a nonexistent threat under OS X. The larger risk is people themselves: Someone downloads what looks to be a legitimate piece of software and installs it, giving up administrator access and opening the computer up to all sorts of problems.

Apple is addressing this vector of attack with Gatekeeper, a sentry that attempts to slam a portcullis between unapproved applications and OS X. In the Security and Privacy preference pane, you'll find an option in the General settings to allow which applications to be installed:

- **Mac App Store.** Apple verifies everything sold through the Mac App Store, so this is the most secure option. Only apps you purchase from the store can be installed.

- **Mac App Store and identified developers.** This option, the default, allows everything from the Mac App Store as well as apps created by developers who have registered and been approved by Apple.

- **Anywhere.** The third option is the same as OS X before Mountain Lion: Install anything as long as you provide an administrator password. (It's up to you to determine what's legitimate or not.)

Gatekeeper is an admirable step, but it's not perfect. It scans applications only when they're installed or launched, and assumes that everything on your computer is already safe. Also, if you receive an app from a friend directly (such as via email, AirDrop, or Dropbox), OS X doesn't perform a Gatekeeper check. Still, with malware proliferating in the world, it's good to have at least this much protection.

Update Applications

Software is rarely perfect when it's released. Bug fixes, security updates, and other issues crop up, which is why you'll need to install updates from time to time. Under Mountain Lion, software updates come through the Mac App Store (a change from Lion and earlier, which had a separate system update mechanism).

Mac App Store

When an update is available for any system component or application you purchased through the Mac App Store, a number appears on the store's icon in the Dock and on the Updates button in the store (**Figure 3.32**). You can also manually check for updates by clicking the Updates button in the Mac App Store or by choosing Software Update from the Apple menu.

Figure 3.32
Mac App Store updates available

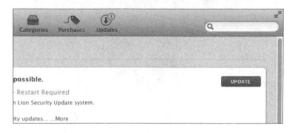

To update an app, click the Update button to the right of the app's name, and enter your Apple ID password if requested.

You can also click the Purchases button at the top of the window and scan through the list of apps you've bought to find ones with Update buttons.

 tip   If an update or purchase was interrupted, choose Store > Check for Unfinished Downloads to resume the download.

Some files get special treatment: necessary system files and security updates are downloaded and automatically installed when you restart the computer. If you'd prefer to handle that manually, go to the Software Update preference pane and turn off the option labeled Install system data files and security updates.

tip To prevent Software Update from downloading anything without your say-so, turn off the option to Download newly available updates in the background in the preference pane.

Updaters within applications

Most applications now have the capacity to check if newer versions are available. Look for a Check for Updates item in the application menu or Help menu. In some cases, you'll be taken to the company's Web site to download the latest version; see "Install Applications," earlier. Other programs can update themselves while they're still running (**Figure 3.33**).

Figure 3.33
An update available within an application

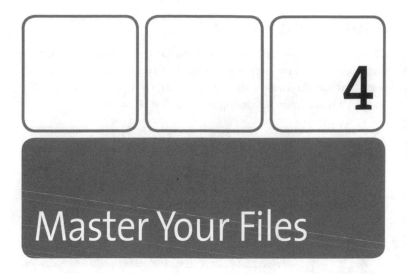

4

Master Your Files

In my years of using and teaching about the Mac, I've run across people who are quite adept in some areas, like using a particular program, but lack some core knowledge about how the computer works. It's as if they missed the first day of a "How to Use Your Mac" class and never caught up with their homework. Ask them to build a spreadsheet in Excel and it's no problem; ask them to locate that Excel file and they're utterly lost.

It's not their fault. No one ever said, "Go learn how a hierarchical file-system works." Instead, they learned how to accomplish a specific task—build a spreadsheet, enhance a photo, read email. And in most cases, those tasks involve files. Files are the foundation of working within OS X, and you can make them work to your advantage.

Your Home Folder

OS X is filled with files and folders, but you can ignore most of them. In fact, Apple recommends you not explore the System folder and other areas that contain crucial system files. Instead, OS X gives every user account a Home folder for storing personal files (**Figure 4.1**).

Figure 4.1
Your Home folder in the Finder

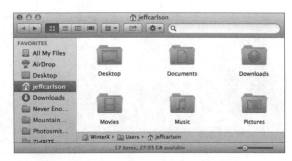

Access the Home folder in the Finder by creating a new window (choose File > New Finder Window, or press Command-N) or by choosing Go > Home (Command-Shift-H). You can also click your account name in the sidebar of any Finder window.

While the Desktop, Documents, Movies, Music, and Pictures folders can hold any type of file, a few of the other folders have specific uses. Downloads is a convenient catch-all location for files downloaded from the Internet or transferred using AirDrop (see Chapter 8). Sites is designed for building and sharing Web sites.

tip The Arrangement button (⊞▾) in the toolbar of every Finder window enables you to arrange the files by criteria such as date modified or size, or to group by application.

tip Longtime OS X users may notice something missing in Figure 4.1: the Library folder. For Mountain Lion, Apple chose to hide the Library folder, presumably to prevent people from accidentally editing or deleting important files used by the operating system. The folder isn't gone, though. To access it, hold Option and click the Go menu in the Finder—Library shows up in the list.

Aside from those exceptions, the Home folder is yours to use. Feel free to create new folders (choose File > New Folder, or press Command-Shift-N) or stash other files here; it all depends on your level of organizational tolerance. (I like to stick to the basics and avoid clutter—a huge surprise considering the disheveled state of the physical desk in my office.)

tip Don't rename or move the folders in your Home folder. Many applications (especially Apple's) store files there. For example, iTunes keeps your music library in a subfolder within the Music folder; if you move it, you could lose track of your songs and videos. (However, you *can* choose to relocate the iTunes library; see Chapter 7 for details.)

Move and Copy Files

Although the Home folder offers locations for common file types, you can store files and folders nearly anywhere. Getting them there is easy.

1. Open two new windows: one containing the item you want to move or copy, and one for the location where you want the file to end up.

2. To *move* a file, click and hold the mouse button, then drag the file to a new destination.

   To *copy* a file to the destination, hold the Option key as you drag; a plus sign (+) icon appears on the cursor to indicate a copy is being made (**Figure 4.2**, on the next page).

3. Release the mouse button to complete the move.

tip If you drag a file between two volumes (such as between two hard disks, or to a hard disk from a networked computer), the file is automatically copied. You can move the file instead, deleting the original copy, by holding Command as you drag.

Figure 4.2
Copying a file

Copy icon

tip Another way to copy a file is to select it and choose Edit > Copy. Switch to the destination and then choose Edit > Paste Item.

Share Files

In Mountain Lion, the new Share button in every Finder window gives you the opportunity to act on one or more files without leaving the window. With a file selected, click the Share button to reveal a menu of options (**Figure 4.3**).

Figure 4.3
The Share menu

The options change depending on the file; for example, the Twitter and Flickr options do not appear if you choose to share a spreadsheet.

 These options are also available from the contextual menu. Right-click or Control-click a file and select an action from the Share submenu.

Delete Files

Discarded files go to the Trash, which, unlike other folders in the Finder, exists on the Dock. Here's how to delete something.

1. Select the offending item in question.

2. Drag it to the Trash icon in the Dock (**Figure 4.4**).

 That said, I almost never drag anything to the Trash. It's much easier to select an item and press Command-Delete to send it to the bin.

Figure 4.4
Dragging a file to the Trash

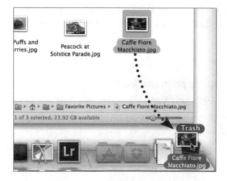

Recover trashed items

If you need to pull something out of the Trash, simply click the Trash icon to display its contents in a new window, and then move the file out. Or, you can select the item in the Trash window and choose Put Back from the File menu or the contextual menu.

Empty the Trash

Although you may have thrown something in the Trash, the item still takes up space on your hard disk. If you're certain you don't need the bits in the bin, empty the Trash in one of the following ways.

- Choose Finder > Empty Trash. OS X will ask you to verify that you really want to do it; click the Empty Trash button.

- Open the Trash and click the Empty button in the upper-right corner of the window.

- Control-click or right-click the Trash icon and choose Empty Trash from the contextual menu that appears.

- Press Command-Shift-Delete in the Finder.

 If you're using Time Machine to back up your data, you can easily recover items you've accidentally deleted. See Chapter 9.

Securely empty the Trash

Even after you've emptied the Trash, the files you deleted are still read-able to file-recovery software. (On the disk, files are only marked as deleted, freeing up their space to be overwritten later.) To ensure that no one can recover the files, securely empty the Trash by choosing Finder > Secure Empty Trash. OS X replaces the files on disk by writing random data to their locations.

 To empty the Trash without being asked to confirm your action, hold Option when you choose Finder > Empty Trash, or press Command-Option-Shift-Delete.

Finder Essentials

The following features have one thing in common: When they were first introduced, I thought they were just eye candy or of limited real use. Boy was I wrong—I now use them all the time.

Quick Look

Select a file in the Finder and press the spacebar. A new window appears with a preview of the file's contents, so you don't need to open the file to tell what it is (**Figure 4.5**). You can view photos, video, audio clips, PDF files, Microsoft Word documents, Keynote presentations, and more. The Quick Look preview floats above your other windows—you can select other items to preview them without closing the Quick Look window.

Figure 4.5
*A Quick Look
view of a PDF file*

tip   Download Quick Look plug-ins that extend the feature to viewing the contents of folders, archives, and file formats not included in OS X at www.quicklookplugins.com.

A Quick Look window also offers more options (**Figure 4.6**).

■ When multiple files are selected, use the arrows (or arrow keys) to move between them.

■ Click the Index Sheet button to view all the files in a grid.

■ Click the "Open with" button to launch the suggested application. Or, right-click the button to view a list of other compatible programs; the list can also include actions, such as "Add to iPhoto" for images.

■ Click the Share button to share the current image via email, Messages, AirDrop, or photo sites.

■ Click the diagonal arrow icon to present the content full-screen.

Figure 4.6
Quick Look options

In Full Screen mode, a few other options appear (**Figure 4.7**).

■ When more than one item is selected for Quick Look, click the Play button to start playing a slideshow of the items.

■ If you're viewing an image, click the Add to iPhoto button to add the photo to your iPhoto library.

■ Click the Exit Full Screen button or press the Esc key to go back to the Quick Look window.

Figure 4.7
Quick Look full-screen options

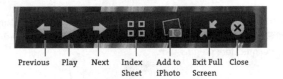

Spring-loaded folders

When you're copying or moving a file or folder, you must do a little bit of prep work by making sure the source and the target are both in visible windows. Spring-loaded folders enable you to grab an item and move it to a folder that may not be visible.

Drag the item onto the top of a folder, wait a moment, and that folder opens automatically. You can keep exploring in this way until you find the intended destination folder. If you opened the wrong folder, move the item (all the while keeping the mouse button pressed) out of the window that sprang open.

A similar effect works with open windows, too. If just a corner of a window is peeking out among dozens of open windows on your screen, that's fine: Drag the file or folder to that window corner to bring the window forward, where you can drop the item to move it.

Create an archive

When you need to send several files to someone over the Internet, it's best to wrap them up into a single package that gets transmitted. Select the files and choose File > Compress *(number of items)*. OS X makes copies and stores them in a .zip archive file.

Find Files with Spotlight

Spotlight is wired deep into OS X and is used by applications such as Mail and the built-in Help system. Whenever you save a change to a document, Spotlight updates its index in the background.

You don't need to do anything to activate Spotlight; it's just there. Occasionally you may notice the Spotlight icon (in the right corner of the menu bar) displaying a pulsating dot, which indicates that Spotlight is indexing new material.

Perform a Spotlight search

There are two entry points for Spotlight in the Finder: the Spotlight icon on the menu bar (which is available in all applications) and the Search field in a window's toolbar.

Search from the Spotlight menu

The idea behind Spotlight is that it's quick and unobtrusive. The Spotlight icon in the menu bar is my first stop for searching.

1. Click the Spotlight icon or press Command-spacebar.

2. Start typing what you're looking for. Spotlight begins to display results as you type.

tip Hover the mouse pointer over an item in the Spotlight results list to view a Quick Look preview of the item (Figure 4.8). You can even watch videos by clicking the Play button that appears in the middle of the preview.

Figure 4.8
A Spotlight
search from
the menu bar

3. If you see what you're looking for, click its name to open it (or use the arrow keys to select it and press Return). The Top Hit is always automatically selected, so you can often just start typing and press Return to jump to the item.

If you don't spot a match, click or select Show All in Finder to view the results in a Finder window (see the next section).

tip Need to make a quick calculation? Enter it in the Spotlight menu, using an asterisk (*) to multiply and a forward-slash (/) for division. So typing "52*45" reveals the answer (2340) within the search results—you don't even need to launch the Calculator application.

tip At the bottom of the Spotlight menu, you'll find Search Web and Search Wikipedia items; select one to expand the search beyond your computer.

Search within a Finder window

Performing a search within a Finder window gives you more options—and more results—than the menu bar.

1. In any Finder window, enter your search term in the Search field. Or, choose File > Find to activate the Search field in the active window (or to open a new window if one wasn't already open). As with the menu bar, results begin to appear as soon as you start typing.

2. Narrow your search, if necessary, by specifying additional search criteria (**Figure 4.9**). Click This Mac to search the entire computer; click "*folder name*" to limit the search to just the active folder; or click Shared to scan shared disks and connected network volumes.

Figure 4.9
A Spotlight search in a Finder window

Normally a search looks through the contents of all indexable files on your computer, but you can limit the query to just file and folder names by choosing the "Filename contains" item from the menu that appears as you type.

3. To further narrow the search, click the plus sign (+) icon on the search bar to apply additional criteria (**Figure 4.10**).

Figure 4.10
Use search criteria to narrow the list.

> **tip** The criteria pop-up menu includes a tantalizing Other item that's worth exploring. Choosing it brings up a window with all sorts of criteria, such as fonts used in a document, specific camera settings for images, and much more. Enable the In Menu checkbox for any item you use frequently.

Advanced Spotlight Searches

Spotlight is capable of performing advanced searches, if you know what to enter. Here's a taste of some possibilities; more information can be found in Apple's Mac Help on your computer.

- Include exact phrases in quotation marks ("jeff carlson").

- Use Boolean operators to combine search terms. Spotlight recognizes AND, OR, NOT, and a minus sign (–), which means AND NOT (Jeff NOT Geoff).

- Specify metadata (such as "kind:images"); Mac Help includes a list of valid keywords.

tip If you find yourself frequently changing the search location, you can set a different default. Choose Finder > Preferences and click the Advanced button in the Finder Preferences window. Select an option from the pop-up menu labeled "When performing a search": Search This Mac, Search the Current Folder, or Use the Previous Search Scope.

Hide data from Spotlight

Spotlight builds its index from everything on your hard disk, but you may want to exclude data such as personal correspondence or financial documents from casual searches. Or, you may have a secondary hard disk being used as a scratch disk to shuttle temporary files for an application like Photoshop or Final Cut Pro.

1. Open the Spotlight preference pane in System Preferences.

2. Click the Privacy button.

3. Drag the folder or hard disk to the list area (**Figure 4.11**). Or, click the Add (+) button below the list and locate the item to exclude.

Figure 4.11
Exclude data from Spotlight's bright glare.

Spotlight helps you quickly find things on your computer. Spotlight is located at the top right corner of the screen.

Search Results   Privacy

Prevent Spotlight from searching these locations:
Click the Add button, or drag a folder or disk into the list below.

Daydreams_Dupe_Remote
My Private Files

tip Too many results? In the Spotlight preference pane, click the Search Results button and deselect any categories you want to hide when you perform searches. For example, you may not want to include Fonts or Web pages.

Smart Folders

Here's where you can really get productive. Not only can you perform searches using multiple criteria, but that search can be saved as a Smart Folder whose contents are updated depending on the search. For example, here's how to set up a Smart Folder that displays documents created in the last week (**Figure 4.12**).

Figure 4.12
*Creating a
Smart Folder*

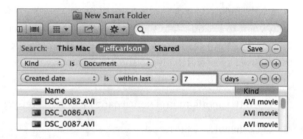

1. Choose File > New Smart Folder to open a new Finder window with the search criteria enabled.

2. Click the plus sign (+) to add a new attribute.

3. Set the Kind attribute to Document.

4. Click the plus sign (+) again.

5. Set that attribute's first pop-up menu to "Created date," and specify that it is within the last 7 days.

6. Click the Save button to save the Smart Folder. Give it a name (and, optionally, a location if you want it somewhere other than Mountain Lion's Saved Searches folder). Make sure the Add To Sidebar checkbox is selected if you want it to appear in the sidebar.

No documents are actually stored in a Smart Folder. Instead, it acts as a portal that filters just the files you want to see, updated live.

5

Manage Important Information

I don't mean to treat computers like people (they hate that, as the saying goes), but there was a time when a computer didn't really care who you were. You'd use a computer for specific tasks: write a letter, balance your checkbook, play games. When you were finished, you'd turn off the computer and do something else.

But now, your Mac running Mountain Lion cares very much about who you are, because computers are more important for our personal lives. We can use Mountain Lion to keep track of friends and acquaintances, schedule events and meetings, and communicate with people all around the world. OS X includes low-level databases for contacts and events that other programs tie into, which helps us manage our lives and synchronize the information between multiple computers and devices, such as the iPhone and iPad.

Synchronize Important Data

These days, it's not enough to have your contacts and events in one place. You want them on your iPhone or iPad, on other computers that you use, and available even when neither of those options is at hand. Apple's iCloud service is built on the idea that your information should appear wherever you are, without you having to manually synchronize it.

You probably also use more than one service for tracking such things, such as Google or a company Microsoft Exchange server. Plenty of possibilities exist for moving that data around and keeping it up to date on your Mac.

Sync data using iCloud

iCloud is free, and Apple is developing it into a service that's as much a part of OS X as the Finder. Your information is stored on Apple's iCloud servers and transferred to your Macs, Windows PCs, and iOS devices. Whenever you edit a record, such as a person's contact information, those changes are delivered to all devices. iCloud also keeps track of notes, Safari bookmarks, email, photos, and documents created by applications that support iCloud. If you haven't yet signed up for an iCloud account, I highly recommend it.

tip Before you enable syncing, make sure your data is backed up. In Contacts, choose File > Export > Contacts Archive. In Calendar, choose File > Export > Calendar Archive. Perform this step in addition to any backup system you have in place, just to be sure.

Open the iCloud preference pane and sign in using your member name and password. Then, select the services you want to sync (**Figure 5.1**). Do the same on other computers and iOS devices, using the same iCloud account name and password.

Figure 5.1
*The iCloud
preference pane*

Roughly speaking, you don't need to do much more with iCloud (which
is the point). However, you do have the option of managing how your
account's 5 GB of storage space is used.

1. Click the Manage button at the bottom of the preference pane.

2. Select an application at left (**Figure 5.2**).

3. To delete an item, where possible, select it and click the Delete button.
   Or, click Delete All to remove all data for that application.

Figure 5.2
*Managing
iCloud storage*

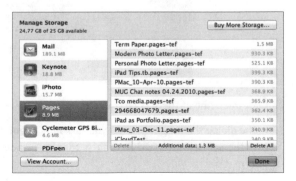

Set up Internet accounts

iCloud is just one of several Internet accounts supported by OS X. Mountain Lion's location for managing all of your Internet accounts is the descriptive Mail, Contacts & Calendars preference pane. From there you can set up which items are accessed by Mail, Contacts, Calendar, and other applications that synchronize that data.

Do the following to set up a new Internet account. If you set up an existing account, such as iCloud, on your Mac prior to installing Mountain Lion, it should already appear in the Mail, Contacts & Calendars preference pane. To illustrate the steps, I'll set up a new Yahoo account.

1. Open the Mail, Contacts & Calendars preference pane (**Figure 5.3**).

Figure 5.3
The Mail, Contacts & Calendars preference pane

2. Click the name of the service you're setting up.

3. In the dialog that appears, enter your account ID and password, and click the Set Up button. OS X contacts the service and verifies your information.

4. Choose the items you wish to sync by clicking their checkboxes (**Figure 5.4**). Click Add Account to continue.

Figure 5.4
*Choose data
to sync.*

When you've finished, that service's data appears in the appropriate applications. In my example, a new Yahoo group appears in Contacts, a new Yahoo calendar with my user name appears in Calendar, a Yahoo list appears in Messages, and the Yahoo email address appears in Mail.

Edit Internet accounts

If you want to enable or disable features of a service, or edit specific options within a program (such as Calendar), open the Mail, Contacts & Calendars preference pane and select the service name. You can then do any of the following:

■ Click the checkbox of a feature to turn it on or off.

■ Click the Details button if you need to enter a different password or change the label that appears in the left column.

■ Double-click a feature to open the application associated with it (such as Contacts if you double-click Contacts) and edit the settings within the app.

Contacts

The Contacts application (which was called Address Book in earlier versions of OS X) keeps track of personal information about your contacts and also interacts with several other applications: Mail, for example, uses it as the source for storing email addresses; iMovie even taps into Contacts when creating credits in its built-in themes.

Create a new contact

Enter a new record for a person or company.

1. In Contacts, click the Create a new card (+) button (**Figure 5.5**) or choose File > New Card.

Figure 5.5
Creating a new contact

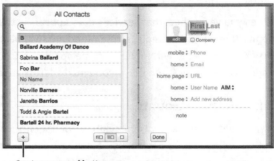

Create a new card button

2. Enter the contact's information in the fields provided. As you do, keep the following techniques in mind:

   ■ When you add information, such as a phone number, to a field, Contacts automatically creates a new blank entry after it, just in case you need to add another number.

   ■ Click the field labels to change them (such as "work" or "home") (**Figure 5.6**).

Figure 5.6
*Changing a
field's label*

Remove field

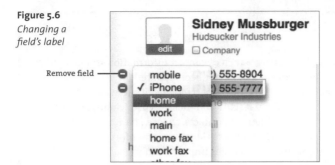

- Click the Remove (–) button to delete any unused fields. However, go ahead and keep fields you think you may fill in later. When you're not editing the card, empty fields are invisible.

- The "user name" field refers to social networking options. Enter the identity and choose a networking service from the pop-up menu, such as Facebook, Skype, and AIM (your iCloud account used by the Messages application).

- To select an image to use, double-click the image field to the left of the contact's name or choose Card > Choose Custom Image. OS X offers a set of Defaults, or you can use your Mac's camera (if equipped) to take a photo. You're then given the option to zoom and position the image as you like. You can also apply effects to the picture by clicking the round Apply an Effect button.

note   What if you want to use an existing photo of someone in the image field? Address Book in Lion offered the ability to select a photo file on disk from within iPhoto or Aperture—but that feature is gone. Instead, do this: Locate the image you want and copy it (choose Edit > Copy). In Contacts, double-click the image field, and then paste the image (choose Edit > Paste).

3. Click the Done button below the card to apply the changes.

Import Contacts

You may already have a bunch of contact information stored digitally in other software that hasn't been updated for years. In the other application, export the contacts to one of these formats: vCard, LDAP Interchange Format (LDIF), tab-delimited, or comma-separated value (CSV) formats. Then, in Contacts, choose File > Import to bring them in. Choose Help > Contacts Help for more information, including ways to ensure that text files import cleanly.

 When entering phone numbers, don't worry about including dashes or parentheses—Contacts formats the field automatically.

Edit a contact

To edit an existing contact's information, select the card in the list and click the Edit button or choose Edit > Edit Card (Command-L).

Add a new field

Contacts offers many more field types than are initially shown, such as middle name, maiden name, and birthday. Choose Card > Add Field and choose from the options that appear.

That menu also includes an Edit Template option, which takes you to the program's preferences. Choose which fields appear for new contacts, then close the preferences window.

 Contacts is also a label- and envelope-printing secret weapon. Choose File > Print and you'll find all sorts of templates and options for printing your addresses.

Data Detectors

Part of the drudgery of handling all of the addresses and phone numbers and email addresses these days is getting them into an organizational tool like Contacts. Mountain Lion makes it easier using data detection technology, which looks through text to find common patterns—such as the formatting of mailing addresses and phone numbers.

In a program that supports data detectors, such as Mail, position your pointer over an address; you'll see a dotted line appear. Click the attached pop-up menu and choose Create New Contact or Add to Existing Contact to send the address to Contacts (**Figure 5.7**).

Figure 5.7
Data detection in action

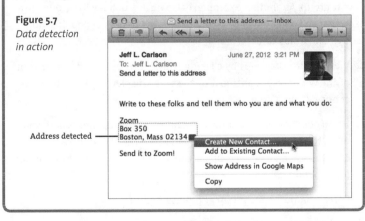

Address detected

The Contacts application can take advantage of the fact that OS X features built-in support for social networks like Twitter and Facebook by pulling information from those sources to fill out contact information. Go to the Mail, Contacts & Calendars preference pane, click an account (such as Twitter), and then click the Update Contacts button. User images and other information is added to cards whose email or account name matches.

Specify your card

When you install Mountain Lion from scratch, the information you provide during the setup process is added to a card in Contacts, which becomes *your* card. To change which card identifies you, select a contact and choose Card > Make This My Card.

Organize contacts into groups

Creating groups in Contacts fulfills that small part of me that likes to impose some order, making it easy to narrow the contact list to just family members or restaurants. But groups are also practical: In Mail, you can type a group name in the To field to send a message to each person in that group. As another example, I also have a holiday list group I use each year so I don't have to come up with the names of people who receive Christmas cards.

1. View the list of groups by clicking the Groups button at the bottom of the window (the leftmost of the three display mode buttons), or choose View > Groups.

2. Hover the mouse pointer over the name of the location where you want the new group to appear, such as On My Mac or iCloud, and click the Create a new group (+) button; or, choose File > New Group (Command-Shift-N).

3. Enter a name for the group and press Return.

4. Click the All Contacts group to view your list of contacts.

5. Drag contacts from the Name column to the name of the group you created. (Contacts can appear in multiple groups.)

tip　With a group or contact selected, press the Option button. Any groups containing the selected contact or any contacts within a selected group are highlighted in blue.

Smart Groups

Because Contacts is really a database of raw information, that data can be scanned for your benefit. Smart Groups let the program perform live stored searches. For example, here are the steps to create a Smart Group that lists all family members whose birthdays are coming up in the next 30 days.

1. Choose File > New Smart Group (Command-Option-N), or click the Create new group (+) button to the right of the Smart Groups heading.

2. Enter a name for the group.

3. Start entering search conditions using the pop-up menus that appear; click the Add (+) button to the right to add more criteria (**Figure 5.8**).

   Also set whether *all* or *any* of the conditions must be met to include a contact in the group using the pop-up menu just below the name.

Figure 5.8
Don't forget upcoming birthdays.

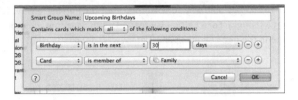

4. Click OK to create the Smart Group, which automatically adds any matching contacts.

   To change the criteria later, select the group and choose Edit > Edit Smart Group; or, right-click the group and choose Edit Smart Group from the contextual menu.

 After you perform a search and want to go back to the results later, choose New > New Smart Group from Current Search. This feature is

helpful if you frequently find yourself looking for all contacts within a certain company, for example.

 To easily share information with someone, select a contact and click the Share button. It sends a vCard containing the particulars.

Delete contacts

To remove a contact from Contacts, select it and press the Delete key or choose Edit > Delete Card. If the contact is in a group and that group is selected, a dialog appears asking if you want to just remove the contact from the group, or delete the contact entirely. If you select a group and press Delete, however, only the group is removed; all of its contacts remain in the database.

 I must admit that the Contacts application has always frustrated me. Some changes under Mountain Lion are welcome—displaying groups in a more sensible way, for example—but the app has always felt like an OS X afterthought. For a better way to work with your contact information, I recommend the free Cobook application (www.cobookapp.com).

Calendar

If I don't write down an event, I won't know about it. It's embarrassing (especially when the event was my mother's birthday—true story). So now I try to store as much time-based information as I can in Calendar (**Figure 5.9**), which gets synchronized to my iPhone and other machines.

Create a new calendar

Unlike the printed calendar you may have in your kitchen, Calendar can display events from multiple calendars. This capability helps you separate types of events (work versus home, for example, or specific projects).

1. Choose File > New Calendar (Command-Option-N).

2. Enter a name for the calendar and press Return.

 tip Select a calendar and choose Edit > Get Info (Command-I) to change its color and make its events stand out among the others in your schedule.

Figure 5.9
Calendar and its view controls

View calendars   New event   View   Previous   Next

Create a new event

Mountain Lion uses a clever Quick Event feature that makes it easier to create new events.

1. Choose File > New Event (Command-N), or click the New Event button. A Create Quick Event dialog appears (**Figure 5.10**).

Figure 5.10
Creating a new Calendar event

2. Enter a description of the event as you would speak it. For example, "Lunch with Kim on Thursday" or "Coffee with Glenn on 7/12 at 2pm" creates events on those dates and times. If you don't specify a time, Calendar usually assumes the current time; in the example above, however, Calendar figures that "lunch" will start at noon.

3. In the new event's description that appears, adjust any of the information, such as location, time, and so forth.

> **tip** Choose Edit > Show Inspector to bring up a separate window that displays the details for any selected event. Otherwise, you need to double-click each event to learn more about it.

Edit an event

To edit an existing event, do one of the following:

- Select an event and choose Edit > Edit Event (Command-E).

- Double-click an event, and then click the Edit button. The event's details appear (**Figure 5.11**).

Figure 5.11
Edit an event's time and other details. Notice that Calendar filled in the Location field based on what I typed when creating the event.

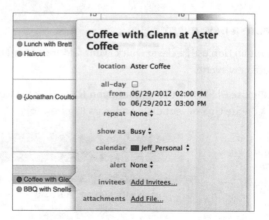

Invite people to events

Whether you're setting up a group meeting or confirming a dinner date, Calendar includes the option to invite people to events.

1. In the event editing window, click the Add Invitees link. A field appears where you can type the names of contacts (if they're in your Contacts), or you can enter email addresses.

2. Click Done. Calendar sends an email message to your attendees.

Review an invitation

If you're on the receiving end of an invitation, follow these steps.

1. You'll receive an email containing an .ics file attachment; double-click the file to open it in Calendar and add it to the calendar.

2. Double-click the event, which appears as a dotted outline.

3. Choose to Accept or Decline the invitation, or click Maybe to acknowledge that you received the invitation but haven't made up your mind (**Figure 5.12**).

Figure 5.12
Respond to an event invitation.

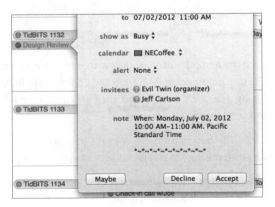

Share calendars

I use several calendars in the Calendars application, including one that my wife and I share to keep track of family events. By sharing a calendar, we both stay up to date on what's going on.

1. Click the Calendars button to reveal the Calendar List.

2. Select the calendar you want to share.

3. Choose Edit > Share Calendar.

4. In the dialog that appears, choose to share the calendar with Everyone (read-only, open to anyone with the address) or to select people you choose (which allows them to edit events) (**Figure 5.13**).

Figure 5.13
Share a calendar.

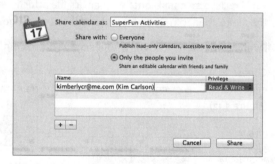

5. Click the Add (+) button or click within the field to add a new person. The app pulls information from the Contacts application, so start typing a person's name to get their email address. Repeat for other folks you want to share with.

6. Choose an option from the Privilege pop-up menu to determine whether the person can edit events (Read & Write) or just view them (Read Only).

7. Click Share to share the calendar.

The recipient of your invitation receives an email asking if they want to share their calendar. When they accept, the calendar appears in the Calendar List on both computers.

> **tip** You may have noticed a curious omission in Calendar: It doesn't include holidays! A calendar without holidays is...well, it's a freelance writer's life, but enough about me. You can certainly create a new calendar and add national holidays, but there's an easier way. Plenty of free calendars are available online, covering holidays, sports schedules, movie release dates, and more; see www.apple.com/downloads/macosx/calendars/. When you locate one, choose File > New Calendar Subscription and enter its URL in the field provided.

Notes

You'd think the digital age would make obsolete all the little scraps of paper we jot notes onto, but I still find myself writing snippets. With the addition the Notes application for OS X, however, all my scribbles now sync with iCloud, so I can find them easily no matter what device I'm on.

The Notes application is simple to use: Click the Add new note (+) button and begin typing. The first line of text becomes the note's title, which appears in the list at left (**Figure 5.14**).

Figure 5.14
The Notes application

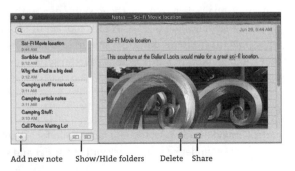

Add new note   Show/Hide folders   Delete   Share

If you want a specific note to remain visible—say, if it contains information you frequently need to reference—double-click the title to pull the note into its own window. You can also choose Window > Float on Top to ensure that other applications' windows don't cover it up.

> **tip** As you can see in the figure, notes can include photos or other files—just drag them onto the note from the Finder. You can also add special formatting such as numbered or bulleted lists by choosing options under the Format menu.

To increase your level of organization, create folders by choosing File > New Folder, or click the Show Folders button and click the Add Folder (+) button to the right of the account name. Then drag notes to the new folder name.

> **tip** I'm using iCloud as the example here, but other accounts support notes, too. Choose Notes > Accounts, or go to the Mail, Contacts & Calendars preference pane and enable notes for any accounts you've set up.

Reminders

Until recently, the iPhone, iPad, and iPod touch lacked a built-in to-do list app. Apple finally delivered one called Reminders with iOS 5 and now extends the application to OS X. What's cool about Reminders, other than being able to sync items between devices, is some of its other features. For example, you can specify that a reminder sounds an alert at a specific date and time, or that it goes off when you reach a certain destination.

Create a reminder

In the Reminders app, click the Add new reminder (+) button, choose File > New Reminder, or simply click within the list and start typing.

To edit the reminder's details, click the "i" button that appears when you move the mouse pointer over an item (**Figure 5.15**). In the dialog that appears, you can set a priority or add a note, as well as specify when the reminder should occur: Select On a Day, At a Location, or both. If you set a location, enter the name of a place to look it up in your Contacts list.

When you've completed an item, click its checkbox.

Figure 5.15
*Editing details
of a reminder*

Add new reminder

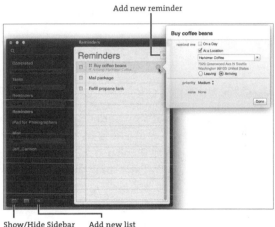

Show/Hide Sidebar   Add new list

note   Setting a location isn't as interesting if you're using Reminders on a desktop Mac, but it is compelling when the reminder is synced to an iOS device or laptop computer that has Location Services enabled. When the device comes within range of a location, or leaves a location, it pops up a notification. For example, you could remind yourself to buy ice cream when you reach the store, or to pick up the dry cleaning after you've left your house.

tip   Another great aspect of Reminders is that it recognizes natural language input. So, typing (or dictating) "Pick up kids at 4:00 tomorrow" correctly creates a "Pick up kids" reminder set to 4 p.m. tomorrow.

Create a new reminders list

Click the Add new list (+) button in the sidebar to create a new list of reminders. If you have multiple accounts set up to use reminders, choose one from the pop-up list that appears.

> **tip** Since Reminders can assign dates to items, you may find it helpful to view them by date instead of by list. Click the Show Calendar button in the sidebar or choose View > Show Calendar and click a date to view items due on that day; a dot appears in the calendar when items are scheduled. You can also choose View > Go to Today (or press Command-T) to jump to today's date.

Work with Text

In terms of raw information, we probably deal with text more than anything else, in a variety of guises. OS X includes many built-in text features that are used by third-party applications. This section is a look at common elements you're likely to encounter, using Apple's included word processor TextEdit as an example (**Figure 5.16**).

Figure 5.16
Common text-editing tools

TextEdit document

Colors window

Substitutions window

Fonts window

- **Fonts window.** In TextEdit, choose Format > Font > Show Fonts. The Fonts window sets typefaces, text size, and an array of formatting.

- **Colors window.** Select something, such as a range of text, and click the color picker in this window to set that color. Drag frequently used colors to the row at the bottom.

- **Substitutions window.** This window contains options for replacing text, such as substituting smart (curly) quotes when you type a straight quote (the default). Click the Text Preferences button to define more substitutions in the Language & Text preference pane.

- **Automatic text correction.** Taking cues from the iPhone and iPad, Mountain Lion now does iOS-style auto-correction of text as you type. When a word looks to be misspelled, Mountain Lion displays an alternate (**Figure 5.17**).

Figure 5.17
Automatic text correction

Continue typing to accept the change (pressing the spacebar or punctuation applies it), or click the X on the alternate to stick with what you've typed. Automatically corrected words appear with a blue dotted underline. If you want to return to what you originally typed, right-click the word and choose Change Back to "*the original word*."

To disable this feature, open the Language & Text preference pane, click the Text button, and deselect the checkbox for "Correct spelling automatically."

- **Dictionary.** OS X includes a complete dictionary you can use for looking up words or for spell-checking documents. The easiest way to look up a word is to start typing it in the Spotlight menu bar field, then select the definition that appears as one of the search results. (You can also launch Dictionary from the Applications folder.)

To spell-check a document in TextEdit, choose Edit > Spelling and Grammar > Show Spelling and Grammar. You can also choose the next item down, Check Document Now, to highlight any misspellings.

 To view the definition for a word in the text, press Command-Control-D over the word in question (Figure 5.18).

Figure 5.18
The inline dictionary

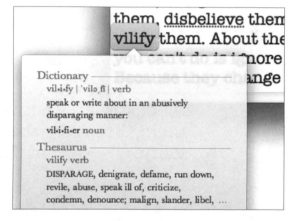

- **Dictation.** On the iPhone, Siri gets a lot of attention not just for its ability to understand natural-language queries and deliver results, but also for its voice dictation feature. You speak, and your words become text. Mountain Lion now supports voice dictation in any text field.

  To start dictation, press the Fn key twice on Macs that include that key (like laptops), or choose Edit > Start Dictation. (You can change the key in the Dictation & Speech preference pane.) A microphone icon appears, indicating that the Mac is listening (**Figure 5.19**).

Figure 5.19
Dictation

Speak in a normal tone of voice, and specify punctuation where needed ("Dear Jane comma sorry I haven't written recently period new paragraph"). When you're done speaking, click the Done button or press the Return key. Mountain Lion sends the audio to Apple for processing—its powerful data centers can analyze the data faster than your Mac—and then enters the text. Although the transcription isn't always perfect, I've been impressed by how well it does.

tip If you have multiple audio input devices, choose which one to use for dictation in the Dictation & Speech preference pane.

Disable the Caps Lock Key

This tip is a matter of personal preference, but I've found that it makes me an overall happier Mac user. If you accidentally hit the Caps Lock key often, as I do, you can disable the key in OS X. Here's how.

1. Open the Keyboard preference pane.

2. Click the Modifier Keys button.

3. In the dialog that appears, set the Caps Lock Key pop-up menu to No Action. Click OK.

Print

The Macintosh has printer toner in its veins, having popularized the first laser printers and started the era of desktop publishing. But printing is still a complicated affair: With many companies creating new models of printers, each with its own special features, printing a simple document can be a tour of dissimilar dialogs and pop-up menus. OS X benefits from decades of work to make the print process easier. As someone who's been there, trust me: You don't want to have to negotiate confusing options just to put ink or toner to paper on a deadline.

Add a printer

If this is your first time printing, or you need to connect to a different printer, the following steps will add a printer for you to use.

1. In any application that can print something, choose File > Print. The Print dialog appears.

2. Click the Printer pop-up menu. Mountain Lion reports if any printers are already on the network; choose one to select it (**Figure 5.20**). OS X communicates with the printer for a few seconds to determine its configuration. You can ignore the rest of these steps and proceed to printing the document.

    If, however, you don't see your printer in the list, choose Add Printer and continue reading.

Figure 5.20
OS X lists connected printers or those on your network.

tip You can also add a printer using the Print & Scan preference pane, but it's just as easy to choose File > Print and set up a printer from there.

3. In the Add Printer dialog, look for your printer in the Default pane; if it's there, select it.

   Your printer may not automatically appear in the list if it uses a different style of connecting, such as over a network. If that's the case, do one of the following:

   ▪ Click the IP button to view options for connecting to a printer that has its own network address (you may need to get this information from a network administrator or consult the printer's documentation). Select the type of communication from the Protocol pop-up menu, then enter the printer's address.

   ▪ Click the Windows button to connect to a printer via SMB/CIFS (the network protocol used by Windows to share printers).

tip Normally, OS X checks to see if it already has driver software for the printer you select. If none is found, or you have troubles printing, click the Use pop-up menu and choose Generic PCL Printer or Select Printer Software and locate the printer model yourself from a list that appears. Or, choose Other from the menu and locate software you may have downloaded from the printer manufacturer's Web site.

Print a document

The printing process generally involves two stages. When you print a document, either the default OS X Print dialog appears or a dialog with custom options for that application appears. After you set the options for that print job (such as deciding which pages to print, for example), the data is sent to the Print Queue, which is an application created just for that printer; you'll see an icon for the printer show up in the Dock. The Print Queue then sends the data to the printer for printing.

Set print options

The steps detailed here represent an overview of print options you're likely to encounter. The software from which you're printing will have more information about specific features.

1. Choose File > Print. You'll probably see the simple version of the Print dialog, which lets you choose a printer and a preset (see "Create a print preset," later in this chapter).

   If that's all the information you need, click the Print button to send the job to the Print Queue.

2. To reveal more print options, click the Show Details button.

3. Set various options for the job, such as the number of copies and which pages to print (**Figure 5.21**). Use the controls below the thumbnail at left to view a small preview of each page to be printed.

Figure 5.21
Advanced printing options

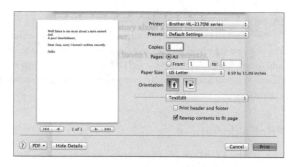

4. Click the unmarked pop-up menu below the standard options to reveal still more settings. Application-specific features appear when the program's name is selected from the menu; you'll also typically find access to the following panes (there are more, but these are the ones you'll probably use most often):

- **Layout.** Choose how many pages are to be printed on each sheet of paper, the direction of the page flow on the printout, whether a border is added, and other features related to how the print appears on paper.

- **Paper Feed.** To print on paper that needs to be manually fed or from a specific print tray, choose Paper Feed from the pop-up menu.

5. Click Print to send the job to the printer.

tip If you have more than one printer set up, you can specify which one is the default printer. Open the Print & Scan preference pane and choose a printer from the Default Printer pop-up menu.

The Print Queue

When you send a print job to a printer, OS X adds it to the Print Queue, an application created just for that printer. In the Print Queue window, you can view the jobs waiting to be printed, pause the printer, delete jobs before they're printed, or hold a job to be printed later (**Figure 5.22**).

Figure 5.22
The Print Queue

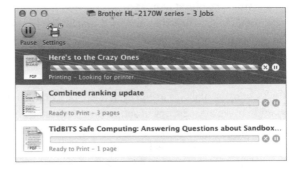

tip Choose Window > Show Completed Jobs to view a list of print jobs that were processed through the queue.

tip Lose track of which jobs are which in a busy print queue? Highlight a job and press the spacebar or choose Jobs > Quick Look (Command-Y) to view a Quick Look preview of the document.

tip If the printer runs into a problem, such as a paper jam, the Print Queue may automatically pause the print jobs. Click the Resume button when the error has been fixed.

Create a print preset

If you often need to print documents with custom settings, such as with a border around each page, create a preset that applies the settings so you don't have to enable them each time.

1. Choose File > Print to open the Print dialog.

2. Apply the print settings you want.

3. From the Presets pop-up menu, choose Save Current Settings as Preset.

4. In the dialog that appears, enter a name for the preset and choose whether the preset applies to all printers recognized by your computer or to just that printer. Click OK. The next time you print, you can choose that preset from the Presets pop-up menu.

Print as a PDF

OS X's print capability is useful even if you don't have a printer or don't want to make a paper copy of something. Because the PDF format is deeply ingrained in the operating system, you can "print" a document to a PDF file. This feature is great for saving receipts of online orders or articles to read later when you may not have an Internet connection.

1. Choose File > Print to open the Print dialog.

2. Click the PDF button, which displays a pop-up menu.

3. Choose Save as PDF.

4. Specify a location for the file, and add metadata such as title, author, subject, and keywords to make the file easier to find later (such as when using a Spotlight search). You can also specify security options: Set a password to open the PDF, to copy content, or to print the document.

5. Click Save to save the PDF to disk.

> **tip** Apparently, someone at Apple wanted an easy solution for saving online receipts. From the PDF pop-up menu, choose Save PDF to Web Receipts Folder. The first time you do this, OS X creates a folder called, appropriately, Web Receipts in your Documents folder. This option saves you the trouble of specifying a location for each receipt.

Save Documents

It's been drilled into us for years: Save your work, and *save often!* Pressing Command-S is now such an automatic action to me that I don't even realize I do it. Apple is trying to eradicate this essential but maddening step with its Auto Save feature. Why should it be our responsibility to save files, when the computer can do it for us?

Applications that have been designed to work with Auto Save write changes to disk almost as soon as you make them—no need to invoke a command at all. (Although, if it makes you feel better, you can still choose File > Save or press Command-S to save manually.) Plus, in coordination with Auto Save, the Versions feature lets you recover older revisions of files (see Chapter 9 for details). However, the change alters the way you work with files. In fact, with the ability to save files to iCloud, Apple hopes you think of "documents" as just more application data, separate from the task of needing to manage files on disk.

Duplicate a file

In applications that do not yet support Auto Save, you can choose File > Save As to create a new copy of an open document and immediately start working on the copy. In applications that do support Auto Save, choose File > Duplicate (Command-Shift-S), which opens a new copy and prompts you to rename it but keeps the original open.

tip If you were frustrated, as I was, that Apple removed the capability to use Save As within an application to make a copy of a file, you'll be happy to know that Apple did listen to feedback. A little. You can now use a keyboard shortcut, Command-Shift-Option-S, to invoke Save As in applications that support the feature.

Documents in the Cloud

Part of the appeal of Auto Save is being able to take advantage of the Documents in the Cloud feature of iCloud. You don't have to worry about where the file is located on disk—it saves to iCloud and is available on all your Macs and iOS devices.

Move a document to iCloud

To save an existing document to iCloud, do the following:

1. Open the file in an application that supports iCloud's Documents in the Cloud feature.

2. Click the document title at the top of the window to view a pop-up menu of options.

3. Choose Move to iCloud (**Figure 5.23**).

4. Click the Move Document button in the confirmation dialog that appears.

Figure 5.23
*Moving a file
to iCloud*

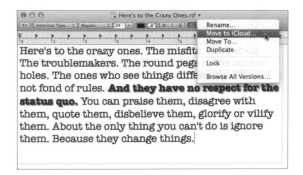

Open a document stored in iCloud

When you want to work on a document stored in iCloud, do this:

1. Launch the application you used to save the document.

2. Choose File > Open (Command-O).

3. In the Open dialog, click iCloud as the source (**Figure 5.24**).

4. Select the file you want and click the Open button.

Figure 5.24
*iCloud option in
an Open dialog*

note Apple's showcase applications for working with documents via iCloud are those in the iWork suite—Pages, Numbers, and Keynote—but as I write this shortly before the release of Mountain Lion, iCloud-enabled versions for the Mac have not yet been released (their counterparts under iOS work just fine). For the time being, you need to employ a workaround: Log in to icloud.com and click the iWork button to view files you've stored at iCloud. Click to download a file to the Mac, and then open it in one of the iWork apps. To share a document back to iCloud, drag it from the Finder to the iCloud.com iWork screen in your Web browser. I expect this situation will change soon, possibly even with the release of Mountain Lion (fingers crossed).

Take Action Using the Services Menu

For most of my time using OS X, I've ignored the Services menu. Apple's intentions were good: Provide a way to share data between applications without going through a lot of hoops. But the Services menu became a long list of unrelated actions. Under Mountain Lion, the mess is gone.

1. Select something—a file in the Finder, or a range of text in a document or in an email message.

2. Choose Services from the application menu. OS X reveals only the services that would apply in that context.

3. Choose an action from the Services submenu to perform it.

Configure services

You can control which services appear. For example, if you never use the Notes feature in Mail, you shouldn't have to always view it as an option.

1. Choose [Application menu] > Services > Services Preferences. The Keyboard preference pane opens, which includes the Services options.

2. Scroll through the list of services and find the one you wish to disable (or enable; not all services are turned on by default).

3. Click the checkbox to the left of the item to disable or enable it.

   If you find yourself using a service often, you can assign a keyboard shortcut for it that works in any application: Double-click the item and then press the keyboard shortcut you want.

4. Close the window to apply the changes.

Create a service in Automator

Using Apple's Automator application, you can create your own services to automate specific tasks.

1. Open Automator and choose Service as the type for a new document.

2. Drag actions from the left column to the right. For example, I created a simple service that takes an image file in the Finder, scales it 50 percent, and adds it to a slide in an open Keynote presentation (**Figure 5.25**).

3. Save the Automator action. It then appears in the Services menu for files that match its criteria.

Figure 5.25
Building a service in Automator

6

Stay in Touch

Having a computer that doesn't connect to the Internet is unthinkable today. And yet, not terribly long ago Apple was advertising how you could easily connect a phone cable to the iMac to get online. Times and technologies have changed (Macs no longer include modems, for example), but the basics of getting connected remain.

Once online, you're exposed to a firehose of information. Send and receive email using Mail; browse the Web with Safari; connect directly to people via Messages; talk to friends and family using FaceTime video conferencing. Mountain Lion includes all the building blocks you need to get online and reach out to the world beyond your computer.

Connect to the Internet

Because Internet access is more pervasive today, most Internet service providers (ISPs) make it easy to get connected. For specifics, refer to the instructions that your ISP gave you when you signed up, but generally an Internet connection works like this:

The ISP provides you with a broadband modem that connects to its servers. Your computer is connected to the modem via Ethernet cable or Wi-Fi networking. The modem then automatically assigns your computer an IP (Internet Protocol) address that enables your service provider to send and receive data.

If, however, you need to manually configure your Internet settings, and you know what you're doing, here's how to access them.

1. Open the Network preference pane (**Figure 6.1**).

2. Choose a connection type from the column at left.

Figure 6.1
The Network preference pane

3. If you're connected via Ethernet, choose a configuration type, such as Manually, from the Configure IPv4 pop-up menu.

   If you're connected via Wi-Fi, first click the Advanced button, then click the TCP/IP button to reach the same settings.

4. Enter the settings provided by your ISP. If you're configuring Wi-Fi, click OK.

5. Click the Apply button to use those settings.

note Networking can be a soup filled with acronyms. Fortunately, Apple keeps much of the terminology away from the casual user. For example, your Internet connection probably uses DHCP (Dynamic Host Configuration Protocol) to assign an IP address. That address likely isn't a unique IP (which are in short supply worldwide) thanks to NAT (Network Address Translation), a technology that gives out local IP numbers as needed.

tip If you frequently take your computer to multiple locations that don't all rely on DHCP, set up location-based profiles that save each spot's networking information. In the Network preference pane, click the Location pop-up menu and choose Edit Locations. Click the Add (+) button to create a new location with the current settings, and then click Done; repeat as needed for the other locations you visit. When you arrive at one of those places, choose Apple menu (🍎) > Location > *location name*.

Join a wireless network

With a laptop and a few bucks in your pocket, nearly any coffeeshop can be your remote office, thanks to wireless Internet access. OS X is smart about wireless networks, asking if you want to join one when you're in range if you're not already connected. You can also choose a network manually, as follows.

1. Click the Wi-Fi icon in the menu bar.

2. Choose a network to use; the icons to the right of the name indicate whether a network requires a password and show the signal strength (**Figure 6.2**).

3. In the dialog that appears, enter the network password and click OK.

Figure 6.2
Connect to a wireless network.

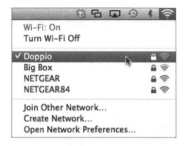

tip Hold Option and click the Wi-Fi menu bar icon to view a host of technical information about the networks, such as which protocols they use, transmit rates, and types of security employed.

note Speaking of coffeeshops, when you connect to a network that requires a sign-in page, a window appears that loads the page so you don't have to open a Web browser first.

Mail

I'm a relative latecomer to Mail, having spent more than a decade relying on Eudora as my email program of choice. When Eudora started to get long in the tooth (and eventually stopped operating under OS X Lion), I chose Mail over other programs. (A big incentive was the way I overhauled my email strategy; see the sidebar "My Approach to Organizing

Email," later in this chapter.) Mail handles email from multiple accounts and provides options for managing it all.

Create a new Mail account

One Mail's great features is its ability to do much of the setup for you if you're creating an email account Mail is familiar with, such as iCloud, Gmail (Google), and Yahoo.

1. In Mail, open the program's preferences and click the Accounts button.

2. Click the Add (+) button at the bottom of the sidebar.

3. Enter your name, email address, and password, and click Continue. Mail contacts the server and fills in all of the appropriate information if possible. (Go to step 5 if this is the case.)

   If Mail can't do it automatically, enter the server information (issued to you by your email provider), in the next screen and click Continue.

note There are two primary email account types. A POP (Post Office Protocol) account checks with the mail server and copies new messages, with options to delete the messages on the server or keep them. IMAP (Internet Message Access Protocol) works a bit differently, keeping your local messages synchronized with the email on the server. Although I relied on POP for years, I've now switched to IMAP for easier access on my iPhone and iPad.

4. On the next screen, enter the outgoing server information given to you by your provider. This is the data needed to send email. If the server requires a password to send messages, select the Use Authentication checkbox. Click Continue.

5. If everything checks out, you're given a summary of the data. You can also enable the account to use Notes, Contacts, Calendars, Reminders, and Messages if you want; the options are selected under the "Also

set up" area of the window. Click Create to take the account online. Your pending messages are delivered and appear in your Inbox.

> **tip** Once an account is set up, more options are available, such as how long messages are stored on the server and how outgoing mail is handled.

> **tip** For a great look at how to use Mail with Gmail accounts, see my colleague Joe Kissell's TidBITS article "Achieving Email Bliss with IMAP, Gmail, and Apple Mail" (http://db.tidbits.com/article/10253).

Read messages

Click a message in the list to view it in the message area (**Figure 6.3**), or double-click to open the message in a new window. If you've set up more than one account, the incoming messages appear together in one mixed Inbox. To view the contents of a single account's Inbox, click the triangle icon to the right of the Inbox toolbar item and choose the account.

Figure 6.3
Reading mail

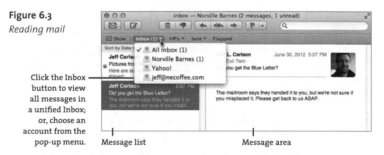

Click the Inbox button to view all messages in a unified Inbox; or, choose an account from the pop-up menu.

Message list   Message area

Apple designed the Mail interface to reduce distractions (and appear more like Mail on the iPad), but I prefer to keep my accounts' folders and Smart Folders visible. To view them, click the Show button just above the message list (**Figure 6.4**).

Figure 6.4
Mailboxes visible

When there are several messages that belong to the same discussion, Mail displays them as a group in the message list and as separate items in the message area (**Figure 6.5**).

Figure 6.5
An email discussion

> **tip** Click the Quick Look URL button that appears when you hover over a Web address in a message to view a preview of the destination.

> **tip** Mail benefits from OS X's Spotlight search technology, enabling you to find messages or text within messages. Type a term in the Spotlight field (or press Command-Option-F to activate the field, and then type) to search your mailboxes. Mail helps by providing additional criteria in a pop-up menu, such as whether to search for the term in Subject lines. When reading a message, press Command-F and start typing to search just within that email.

Compose and send a message

To create a new message, do the following:

1. Click the New Message button on Mail's toolbar, choose File > New Message, or press Command-N. An empty outgoing message appears with the To field active.

2. Start typing the name of a recipient. Mail auto-completes the field using contact information from the Contacts database. (Now you see why I spent time covering Contacts in the previous chapter.) If more than one match is found, choose the one you wish to use.

   Continue adding other recipients, and type a subject too.

3. If you have more than one account set up, choose one from the From pop-up menu. (Optionally, choose an outgoing mail server too.)

4. Type the body of your email in the message field.

5. Click the Send button to dispatch the message, or choose File > Save to save it for sending at another time.

> **tip** Mail is set up to check your spelling as you type, highlighting misspellings with a dotted red underline. To change this behavior, choose Edit > Spelling and Grammar > Check Spelling and choose While Typing, Before Sending, or Never. Mail under Mountain Lion also corrects spelling automatically, making changes as you type (see Chapter 5 for more information).

Add an attachment

To attach a file to an outgoing message, choose File > Attach Files (Command-Shift-A), click the Attach button in the toolbar, or drag a file from the Finder to the body of your message.

> **tip** If you're attaching multiple files, consider packaging them into a .zip archive first and sending that file (see "Create an archive" in Chapter 4).

tip Try not to send large files as email attachments, for two reasons. Each message passes through numerous mail servers on its way to the recipient, leaving a temporary copy at each one; multiply that by millions of people sending attachments, and we're talking about slowdowns in some pockets of the Internet. Closer to home, it's more likely that a message with a large attachment will be marked as possible spam or a virus and won't be delivered.

Reply to a message

To respond to an incoming message, select it and click the Reply button in the toolbar or press Command-R. You can also click Reply in the row of buttons that appears when your mouse pointer rolls over the separator between the header and the message body. The appearance of the outgoing message depends on a few factors.

- If you reply with nothing selected, the contents of the incoming message are included and quoted—indented, colored, and displaying a line on the left edge (**Figure 6.6**).

Figure 6.6
Replying to a message

Quoted text ——

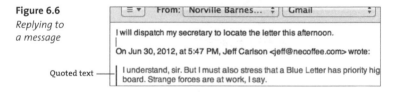

- When you select text in the original message and then reply, only that text is quoted.

- To send a reply to all recipients included on a message, click the Reply All button or press Command-Shift-R.

tip Never, ever hit Reply All without a good reason and without knowing who else is on the list.

note In addition to replying to a message, you can also forward it to some-one else (click the Forward button, or press Command-Shift-F), which quotes the message in the same manner. Another tool I frequently use is Redirect (choose Message > Redirect, or press Command-Shift-E), which sends the message to someone else but keeps the original sender in the From field.

File messages in mailboxes

As your email volume increases, you may want to organize it in some fashion. (Or you may not—I know people who keep all their messages in the Inbox.)

Create a new mailbox

You can set up mailboxes on your Mac or, if you're using an IMAP account, on the server.

1. With the mailbox list visible, choose Mailbox > New Mailbox, or click the Add (+) button at the bottom of the sidebar and choose New Mailbox from the pop-up menu (**Figure 6.7**).

Figure 6.7
*The Add (+)
button pop-up
menu*

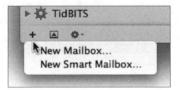

2. In the New Mailbox dialog, specify where the box will reside using the Location pop-up menu.

3. Enter a name for the mailbox, then click OK. The mailbox appears in the sidebar.

File a message

Simply drag one or more selected files from the Inbox (or other mailbox) to the desired mailbox in the sidebar.

> **tip** I far prefer using a keyboard shortcut to file messages, but Mail offers little support. Instead, try Mail Act-On (www.indev.ca). (Also see the sidebar two pages ahead.)

Smart Mailboxes

You'll quickly realize that Smart Mailboxes in Mail are wonderful things, enabling you to view messages that meet specific criteria.

1. Choose Mailbox > New Smart Mailbox, or choose Smart Mailbox from the Add (+) pop-up menu at the bottom of the sidebar if it's visible.

2. Give the mailbox a name and define criteria (**Figure 6.8**). If a message was selected, the To address is included as a starting point. Click the plus (+) icon to the right of a condition to add another.

3. Click OK when you're done.

Figure 6.8
Create a new Smart Mailbox.

Smart Mailbox Name: Attachments last 3 weeks

Contains messages that match [all ⬧] of the following conditions:

Any Recipient ⬧	Contains ⬧	norville.barnes.hud@gmail.com	⊖ ⊕
Date Received ⬧	is in the last ⬧	[3] [Weeks ⬧]	⊖ ⊕
Contains Attachments ⬧			⊖ ⊕

☐ Include messages from Trash
☐ Include messages from Sent   [Cancel] [OK]

> **tip** One thing that makes Smart Mailboxes powerful is the capability to reference other Smart Mailboxes. So you could, for example, create one that displays all mail from a select group of people, then create another that looks for messages in the first mailbox dated within the past week.

VIPs

One problem I have with email is volume: I receive a lot of messages, and sometimes important ones slip by. One way to prioritize email is to mark senders as VIPs (very important persons). Mail ensures that messages from those people don't get tripped up in its junk mail filters, marks those recipients as a VIPs with a star icon, and creates Smart Mailboxes that pull up all messages from them.

To set an address as a VIP, open a message from the person, move the mouse pointer over the person's name, and click the icon that appears to the left.

Later, you can easily locate messages from those folks by clicking the VIPs button in Mail's Favorites bar; click and hold the button to reveal a pop-up menu to choose a specific VIP (**Figure 6.9**).

Figure 6.9
Mail creates a smart mailbox for each VIP.

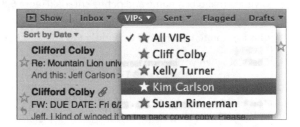

Deal with junk mail

Unsolicited email is a highly annoying but inescapable facet of online communication. Mail includes a built-in junk mail filter that tries to identify the cruft for you.

Sometimes, Mail needs your help. If you receive a junk message, select it and click the Junk button on the toolbar, choose Message > Mark > As Junk Mail, or press Command-Shift-J.

tip Normally, Mail identifies junk mail and leaves it in your Inbox so you can review it. If you're confident in Mail's ability to filter the good from the bad, you can make the junk disappear. In Mail's preferences, click the Junk Mail button and choose, under "When junk mail arrives," the option labeled "Move it to the Junk mailbox." You can open that mailbox at any time to search for good messages that were incorrectly flagged.

tip Mail does a decent job of identifying junk, but I prefer a utility called SpamSieve (c-command.com/spamsieve/), which works within Mail and performs better.

My Approach to Organizing Email

Before I switched to Mail, I filed my messages into dozens of mailboxes (most in nested folders) in Eudora to organize them. It was too much. When my Inbox hit around 700 messages, I just stopped filing.

Now, my system is simple: After I deal with a message in the Inbox, it goes to a single Filed folder. Even better, I can do it with a keyboard shortcut: After a message is dragged to a folder, Mail remembers that location and applies it to the Message > Move to "*mailbox name*" Again menu item (Command-Option-T).

I've set up several Smart Mailboxes for current projects and clients, letting the computer go find the messages for me. For example, a Smart Mailbox called "Mountain Lion Pocket Guide" locates all messages in which my editor, copyeditor, indexer, and production editor are included as recipients.

I no longer need to worry about where to file messages, and I know that the email I need is accessible via a Smart Mailbox or by performing a Spotlight search.

Browse the Web with Safari

The Web is pervasive in today's society, as common a communication medium as television, print, and radio. Apple's Safari Web browser is your built-in window to the Web.

Access Web sites

Use the following techniques to go to Web sites and navigate Safari's interface (**Figure 6.10**).

- Enter a URL into the Smart Search field and press Return to load a page.

- Enter any text in the same field to perform a Google search (in earlier versions of Safari, search was performed in a separate field). Click the magnifying glass icon at the left edge to display recent searches.

- Click the Reload Page button to get the latest version of a page.

- Click the Back and Next buttons to visit sites you've previously viewed during the current session. Or, swipe right or left with two fingers to go back or forward through a window's browsing history.

Figure 6.10
Safari's main components

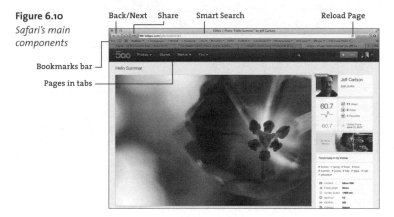

Back/Next   Share   Smart Search   Reload Page

Bookmarks bar

Pages in tabs

tip Maybe it's the higher-resolution screens available today, or maybe it's just my aging eyes, but some text on Web pages is too small to read comfortably. To improve readability, double-tap with two fingers (if you have a trackpad) to zoom in, or choose View > Zoom In (Command-+). To increase just the size of the text, not images or other elements, first choose View > Zoom Text Only and then zoom in.

note Safari is my browser of choice, but I also run Google Chrome (www.google.com/chrome/) and, occasionally, Mozilla's Firefox (www.mozilla.com). Some Web sites use outdated forms or Windows-based software that doesn't play well in Safari but works fine in Firefox. If a Web site isn't working as you expect it to, try loading it in another browser.

Tabs and windows

Each Web page can be loaded into its own window, or you can reduce clutter and load multiple pages in tabs that belong to one window. Safari's settings dictate what content loads in a new tab or window— by default it's Apple's Start page, but you can choose other options in Safari's General preferences.

- Choose File > New Window, or press Command-N, to open a new window.

- Choose File > New Tab, or press Command-T, to open a new tab. You can also Command-click a link on a Web page to open the link in a new tab.

- To turn a tab into a window, drag the tab out of the Tab bar.

- View tabs in a sliding interface by choosing View > Show All Tabs (Command-Shift-\), pinching with two fingers, or clicking the Show All Tabs button to the right of the Tab bar. Then navigate between them by swiping with two fingers or pressing the arrow keys.

tip With several windows open, choose Window > Merge All Windows to collect them all as tabs in one window.

tip Have you ever accidentally closed a window or quit Safari and wanted to get back to the sites you were browsing? Choose History > Reopen Last Closed Window, or History > Reopen All Windows from Last Session.

iCloud Tabs

Since I use several devices throughout the day, I often begin to read something on one machine, then find myself wanting to continue later when I'm using another Mac or my iPhone or iPad. With my iCloud account, I can click the iCloud Tabs button to view which windows and tabs are open on any of my devices (**Figure 6.11**).

(As this book goes to press, iCloud Tabs work only between Macs and Windows PCs. iOS devices will gain the feature when iOS 6 is released.)

Figure 6.11
iCloud Tabs

Bookmarks

I've discovered over the years that I don't use bookmarks much; I tend to collect only a few sites that I want to revisit, and I rely on Google searches or Safari's auto-complete features to pull addresses out of my browsing history. However, I haven't given up on bookmarks entirely. Here's how I add the important ones.

1. Use the Smart Search field to load a Web page.

2. Click the Share button and choose Add Bookmark.

3. Enter a name for the bookmark and choose where it will be displayed.

4. Click the Add button.

Bookmarks can be edited by clicking the Bookmark icon (the book) on the Bookmarks bar.

OS X and Adobe Flash

Starting in 2010, Apple stopped including Adobe's Flash software on new Macs. The company discovered that the leading cause of Safari crashes was Flash content, so now Flash is something you have to install yourself. When you visit a Web page that uses Flash for video or interactive content, you see a message saying you need the latest Flash Player to view it. You can download and install Flash from get.adobe.com/flashplayer/.

However, I suggest you not install Flash. In addition to crashes, it's long been a security vulnerability and uses so much processing power (usually on animated ads that you don't want to view anyway) that it makes the fans in my computer frequently blast at full speed. Instead, install Google Chrome, which includes Flash but keeps it contained within its own application space. When you encounter a Web site that really needs Flash (and the number of those is declining), you can switch to Chrome. Or, install the ClickToFlash Safari extension (hoyois.github.com/safariextensions/clicktoplugin/).

If you already have Flash installed system-wide and want to remove it, follow the steps found at daringfireball.net/2010/11/flash_free_and_cheating_with_google_chrome. You won't regret it.

Here's one bookmark feature I use every day (to check the blogs I manage); it requires a bit of setup, but the payoff is worth it. Choose Bookmarks > Add Bookmark Folder (Command-Shift-N), which creates a new folder in the Bookmarks editing window. Name the folder, then select the Bookmarks Bar item under Collections. Drag the new folder to a new spot in the list of bookmarks in the main area of the window. Finally, add Web sites to that folder. With all that setup out of the way, open a new window and then Command-click the name of the folder in the Bookmarks bar—all your sites are loaded at once into tabs within the window!

Read without distraction

If you encounter an article on a Web page with text that's too small, or that is difficult to read due to layout or color, look for a Reader button at the right edge of the Smart Search field. Clicking it displays the text of the article in a reader-friendly format of large black text on a white background, with no ads in sight. Click the button again to return to the original page.

Reading List

One great thing about living in our connected world is the amount of interesting material to read on the Web. At least a few times a day, people suggest articles to read via Twitter, Facebook, and email. The problem is, I can't drop everything and go read them, especially longer works—I'd never get anything done.

Safari's Reading List feature enables me to save an article (or any Web page) for later, without having to create a bookmark (that I'll forget to delete), or litter my screen with countless browser windows and tabs.

 As of Mountain Lion, Reading List stores the full copy of a Web page so you can still read it later when you're offline, like on an airplane.

To add a page to the list, do one of the following:

- Choose Bookmarks > Add to Reading List (or press Command-Shift-D).

- Click the Show Reading List button in the Bookmarks bar and click the Add Page button (**Figure 6.12**).

Figure 6.12
Add an article to Reading List.

- Drag a link to the Reading List pane or onto the Reading List icon.

- Click the Share button and choose Add to Reading List.

- Shift-click a link.

When you have some time to go back and read, click the Reading List button to view your saved pages, and then click one to load it.

tip   Reading List is pretty slick, but I prefer Marco Arment's Instapaper service (www.instapaper.com) because it allows me to save a clean version of an article. Reading List requires that you first load the page and then click the Reader button.

Download files

When you click a link to download a file, Safari adds the file to the Downloads list, located to the right of the Smart Search field, and deposits it in the Downloads folder within your Home folder. Click the Downloads button to do any of the following:

- Double-click a file to launch it in the application used for that file type.

- Click the Show in Finder button to open the Downloads folder and select the file (**Figure 6.13**).

Figure 6.13
The Downloads window

Show in Finder

- Select a file and press the Delete key to remove it from the list.

- Click the Clear button to remove all downloads; the files themselves remain in the Finder.

> **tip** To extend Safari's functionality, go to Safari > Preferences and click the Extensions button. Click the Get Extensions button and explore lots of cool add-ons that improve the reading and browsing experience.

Messages

Who would've thought instant messaging could become such a big deal for Apple? Messages began as iChat, an interface for sending one-to-one text chats using the AIM (AOL Instant Messaging) network, and has evolved into a dynamic, useful communication tool.

In Mountain Lion, Messages opens the Mac to Apple's iMessage service, which lets you send text messages from iOS devices without being hit with the nonsensical fees that cellular providers charge for SMS texts.

Set up a Messages account

Messages uses your Apple ID for communicating over the iMessage network, and it also supports the AIM, Yahoo, Jabber, and Google Talk services. If you want to send texts solely via iMessage, skip ahead to the next page. To set up one of the latter four services, do the following:

1. In Messages's preferences, click the Accounts button.

2. Click the Add (+) button.

3. Choose the Account Type, enter your screen name and password, and click Done.

tip If you don't want to make your Apple ID email address public, you can set up other addresses for people to use when contacting you. In the Accounts preferences, add addresses in the field labeled "You can be reached for messages at."

Add buddies

If your chat account already exists (for example, you used iChat under Lion), choose Window > Buddies and you'll see all of your buddies in the Buddies window (**Figure 6.14**). If not, you can add friends to the list.

Figure 6.14
Messages Buddies window

1. Click the Add (+) button and choose Add Buddy from the pop-up menu that appears.

2. Enter your buddy's account in the Account Name field. You can also start typing in the First Name and Last Name fields to look up the information from your Contacts list.

3. Click the Add button. Your buddy, if online, appears in the list.

Chat via text message

Chatting via text is a good way to exchange snippets of conversation without the potential delay of sending email. If you're on the receiving end of a chat, an invitation window appears, asking you to accept or decline the message. If you're starting a chat, follow these steps.

1. Click the Compose a New Message button next to the Search field.

2. Start typing the name of the person who will receive your text, and then choose an address to use (**Figure 6.15**).

Figure 6.15
*Choose a
recipient address.*

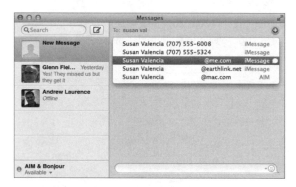

Messages assumes that any phone number is a potential iMessage-capable iPhone, but it doesn't know for sure until you've connected once (in which case, a small blue chat icon appears next to the address). So, if you're sending a message to a friend's iPhone, make sure you're choosing the correct number.

You can also initiate text chats with several people by entering their names in the To field, or by clicking the Add (+) button that appears and choosing from your Contacts list.

3. Type your message in the message area at the bottom of the window (**Figure 6.16**). Your discussion is saved in the column at right.

Figure 6.16
*The beginnings
of a heady
chat session*

Change your status

Messages is an instant service, which means you're likely to get chat invitations at any point. For accounts other than iMessage, if you want to stay connected but would prefer to advertise that you wish to not be disturbed, click the status menu at the lower left of the Messages window (which typically reads "Available") and choose Away or any of the other messages in the list.

tip Setting your status to Away doesn't mean you're unreachable. It's more of a notification to others that you'd prefer not to be disturbed. The Invisible status, however, is another story: You can see your buddies and connect to them, but anyone who counts you as a buddy won't see that you're online.

Audio and video chat

With decent broadband Internet service at each end, you can see and talk to someone on the other side of the world for free. Messages offers two video chat possibilities: the built-in video from its iChat days and an easy handoff to the FaceTime application (covered at the end of this chapter).

> **tip** The person with the best processor and Internet connection should initiate a video chat for best results.

1. In the Messages window, click the Video button at the upper-right corner and choose a FaceTime address your friend uses. Messages launches FaceTime if it's not already running. Jump ahead to the FaceTime discussion, later.

   To start a video chat with someone in your Buddies list, select them in your list; a green icon showing either Messages's audio or video icon indicates your friend's chatting capabilities.

2. Click the Audio or Video chat button at the bottom of the Messages Buddies window, or choose Buddies > Invite to *[Video* or *Audio]* Chat. When the other person accepts the chat invitation, an audio window indicates the connection is open, or they appear onscreen in a video chat window (**Figure 6.17**).

3. When you're finished, close the window to end the chat.

> **tip** If you think an audio or video chat should work but it doesn't, go to Video > Connection Doctor and choose Capabilities from the Show pop-up menu. It will report what's working and what isn't.

> **tip** Get the family together! Depending on your Mac's processing power and your Internet connection, you can chat simultaneously with up to four people over video or ten people over audio.

Figure 6.17
Video chat

Messages Theater

A form of video chatting, the Theater feature lets you display other content aside from your handsome mug on your friend's screen, such as PDF files, photos, movie files, and more. With a video chat active, drag a file to the video window and drop it on the Share with Theater area that appears. The contents of the file becomes what your friend sees (**Figure 6.18**).

Figure 6.18
Sharing photos using Messages Theater

Choose Video > Show Local Video to view the video your camera is sending.

Control someone else's screen

This feature is what helped me convince a couple of family members to finally upgrade their ancient Macs. The screen sharing feature in Messages lets you view *and control* another person's screen (with their approval). It's fabulous for troubleshooting problems that are difficult to describe in email or over the phone.

1. Select a person in your Messages Buddies list.

2. Click the Screen Sharing button at the bottom of the Buddies window and, from the pop-up menu that appears, choose Ask to Share *[buddy's]* Screen.

3. Your buddy's desktop appears, and a thumbnail image of your screen is pushed to a corner; click the thumbnail at any time to switch back to controlling your screen.

   A screen sharing session also acts as an audio chat, letting you speak to each other while you're working on their computer.

FaceTime

We were all supposed to be communicating on video phones by now, right? Well, it turns out that now we can, for real, using FaceTime, which was designed to work with iOS devices too. My toddler never had the patience to sit in front of a computer, but I can follow her around the room with my iPhone or iPad while she chats with the grandparents who are using FaceTime on their Mac.

Set up your FaceTime identity

On the Mac, your Apple ID is the identifier that routes incoming FaceTime calls to the computer. Open the FaceTime application, and enter your

Apple ID and password to set up your identity; or, click Create New Account to set up a new Apple ID.

Make a FaceTime call

FaceTime uses the contact information found in Contacts to connect you with other FaceTime users. Click the Contacts button to reveal your list, and click a person's name to reveal their details (**Figure 6.19**). If this is a person you'll be calling often, click the Add to Favorites button and then click the number or email address they use for FaceTime.

Figure 6.19
FaceTime contact details

To make a FaceTime call, do the following:

1. Locate a person's information by clicking the Favorites, Recents, or Contacts button at the bottom of the FaceTime window.

2. Click a number or email address to start the call.

3. When the other person answers, you're immediately connected. While you're chatting, you can mute your audio, end the call, or switch to full screen by clicking the buttons at the bottom of the screen (**Figure 6.20**).

Figure 6.20
FaceTime controls

tip Choose Video > Use Landscape (Command-R) to rotate the window into a wide view.

4. When you're finished, click the End button to disconnect the call.

Twitter and Facebook

Apple built support for these two popular social networks directly into OS X, enabling you to post updates in areas beyond just the Web or dedicated client applications. For example, Notification Center includes a button for composing a Twitter post, and Twitter appears in Share buttons throughout the system.

To make sure OS X knows about your accounts, go to the Mail, Contacts & Calendars preference pane, click the button for the one you want (such as Twitter), and enter your account information (**Figure 6.21**).

Figure 6.21
Twitter account information

note As this book goes to press, Facebook support is scheduled to appear later in 2012, so don't be confused if you don't see it yet.

7

Enjoy Media

Within an amazingly short amount of time, the bulk of our personal media has gone digital. Although plenty of people still shoot film and buy albums on vinyl, I would guess that most of us now capture images with digital cameras and buy music online or on CDs (which are then converted to digital files).

Apple has long been a champion of digital media—the iTunes Store is arguably saving the music business—so it's no surprise that OS X handles these media requirements. A large reason for that is QuickTime X, the core technology that handles video and audio in OS X. This chapter covers importing digital media into your Mac, as well as using QuickTime Player as a built-in, catch-all solution to view and share it.

Music

iTunes has evolved from a little utility that played MP3 audio files to one of Apple's most important applications.

Import into iTunes

If you already have audio files that you want to add to iTunes, do one of the following:

- Drag the files onto the Music entry under Library, in the iTunes sidebar.
- Choose File > Add to Library (Command-O), locate the files on disk, and click Choose.

You probably already own plenty of music CDs—wouldn't you rather store all that plastic in a box somewhere and listen to the music on your Mac or iOS device? Insert a CD into your Mac's optical drive. iTunes reads the disc and attempts to get track information from an online service. Within a few seconds, iTunes asks if you'd like to import the songs. Click Yes. (You can also opt to not be asked every time, or you can import the tracks manually.)

> **tip** iTunes encodes music into AAC (Advanced Audio Coding) format. To use a different format, open the iTunes preferences, click the General button, and click the Import Settings button. Then, choose another encoder from the Import Using pop-up menu.

Buy from the iTunes Store

I'll be honest: I hadn't purchased a CD for a couple of years before Apple introduced the iTunes Store—I'd been burned by too many albums with one or two good songs and lots of mediocre material. Being able to sample songs in 90-second bursts and, more importantly, buy music and immediately download it to my hard disk rekindled my interest.

1. Click the iTunes Store item in the sidebar to view the online storefront.

2. Locate a song you want to buy, either through browsing or by using the Search field at the upper-right corner of the iTunes window.

3. Click the Buy Album or Buy Song button, enter your personal information, and wait for the files to download.

tip If you own an iOS device, download Apple's free Remote app from the App Store. Remote gives you control over iTunes on a computer on your network. I'll use my home setup as an example: My music collection is stored on a separate computer in another part of the house, which sends the audio to an AirPort Express unit attached to the stereo in the living room. Instead of going into the other room to select music or control playback, I use Remote on my iPhone or iPad to specify which music to play, no matter what room I'm in.

Share iTunes libraries using Home Sharing

Using the Home Sharing feature of iTunes, you can play media from your Mac on several devices without having to copy the files to them. For example, if an album is on your main Mac and you want to listen to it on an iPad or Apple TV, simply stream the audio. Set up Home Sharing by doing the following:

1. In iTunes, choose Advanced > Turn On Home Sharing.

2. Enter your Apple ID (the one you use to buy media from the iTunes Store) and password. Note that all devices using Home Sharing must be configured with that one ID.

3. Do the same in iTunes on any other Macs or Windows PCs on your local network. On an iOS device, go to Settings > Music > Home Sharing and enter the same information.

4. In iTunes, select a shared library in the sidebar, listed under the Shared heading. On an iOS device, open the iPod app, tap the Library button in the sidebar, and choose a shared library.

5. Locate the media you want, and then press Play.

iTunes Match

The iTunes Match service, which is a separate, $24.99-per-year component of iCloud, tackles the issue of multiple devices in a different way. The entire library is available to all of my devices, and unlike Home Sharing, iTunes Match doesn't require them to be on the same network. I can listen to an old album simply by clicking the Play button—it streams from Apple's iCloud servers (**Figure 7.1**). Or, I can choose to download the files so they reside on my computer by clicking the iCloud download button.

Figure 7.1
iTunes Match

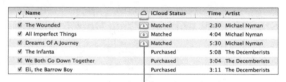

Tracks stored on iCloud

If you choose to subscribe, iTunes gathers information about your library and uploads it to iCloud. Apple compares that data with the songs stored in its master iTunes library and matches them. Any tracks that do not reside at Apple are uploaded so you can access them from anywhere, or recover them if you accidentally delete them.

tip iTunes Match has another great benefit. If you originally ripped songs at a low quality, you can download high-quality replacements for no extra charge. After iTunes Match is set up, delete the songs in iTunes on your Mac (but make sure not to select the option to remove them from iTunes Match), and then click the iTunes Match download button that appears with the track or album.

Choose a Different iTunes Library Location

iTunes puts your media library in your Home folder (specifically, in Music/iTunes/iTunes Music), but that's not always the ideal location. What if your music library is especially large and better served on an external hard disk? To specify an alternate location, do the following:

1. Move your current iTunes Music folder to the new location.

2. Open the iTunes preferences and click the Advanced button.

3. Under the iTunes Music folder location, click the Change button and specify the new directory. Click OK to exit the preferences.

tip It's also possible to work with multiple iTunes libraries. When you launch iTunes, hold the Option key until you see the Choose iTunes Library dialog. Click Choose Library to specify the one you want to use (it's the iTunes Library file one level above the folder where your music files are located), and then click the Choose button. iTunes will automatically open the last-used library, so repeat this technique to switch to your original library.

Digital Photos

Apple's tool of choice for organizing and editing digital photos is its own iPhoto. However, iPhoto isn't the only option: Programs such as Apple's Aperture, Adobe Photoshop Lightroom, or Adobe Photoshop Elements include their own importing tools, but in general the process is similar.

note Mountain Lion does not include iLife, Apple's suite of "digital hub" applications that includes iPhoto, iMovie, and GarageBand. However, iLife is free on every new Mac, or you can buy the apps individually for $14.99 each at the App Store.

Import into iPhoto

Normally, when you connect a camera via USB (or you insert a memory card into a card reader), iPhoto launches and displays its import interface (**Figure 7.2**).

Figure 7.2
iPhoto import

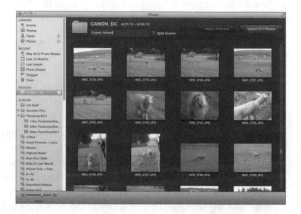

1. Enter something in the Event Name field to categorize this batch of pictures. iPhoto groups photos into Events to help you keep track of them. If you leave this field blank, the program uses the photos' dates as Event names. You can optionally type notes in the Description field.

2. If you wish to import the entire contents of the memory card, click the Import All button. Or, if you want to grab just a few images, select their thumbnails and click the Import Selected button. The photos are copied to your iPhoto library.

3. When iPhoto asks if you want to delete the photos on your camera, click Keep Photos instead. It's better to let the camera format the memory card to its own settings.

note One very cool feature of iCloud is Photo Stream. Any photos you capture or import using an iOS device are automatically uploaded to iCloud and made available to all your devices. iPhoto and Aperture can also tie into Photo Stream, providing an instant import of those shots.

Import into Image Capture

Apple provides another tool for importing photos: Image Capture, located in the Applications folder. If you have a different workflow for importing photos directly to the hard disk, instead of letting iPhoto organize them for you, Image Capture provides a streamlined entry point.

1. Launch Image Capture and connect your camera or media card.

2. Select the device in the list at left; images appear at right.

3. Choose a destination from the pop-up menu below the photos.

tip Two items in that pop-up menu are pretty cool: Build Web Page downloads the images from the camera and creates a basic Web page, which is saved to the Pictures folder. Make PDF, as you would expect, builds a contact sheet. In the Make PDF application that opens, you can also change the layout of the images by choosing options from the Layout menu.

4. Select the photos you want and click Import, or click the Import All button to copy all files.

tip Image Capture has a great feature if you shoot with multiple cameras. When one is connected, you can specify which application (Image Capture, for example, or iPhoto) opens just for that camera. So, connecting your DSLR could launch Image Capture or Aperture, while your compact point-and-shoot camera could trigger iPhoto. This option appears in the lower-left corner of the window; you may need to click the "Show device settings" button in that corner to reveal the option.

Digital Video

iPhoto stores casual video shot by most digital cameras, including the iPhone, because usually those videos are short snippets of footage instead of longer-form video shot by a camcorder (**Figure 7.3**). The clips are imported when you import your digital photos.

Figure 7.3
Photos and movies in iPhoto

Photo   Movie

iMovie

To edit longer sequences of video, turn to iMovie. Like iPhoto, it stores all your videos in one central library; in fact, iMovie also scans your iPhoto library and makes the video clips there available for editing. If you're importing footage from a camcorder, do the following:

1. With iMovie open, connect your camcorder; the Import window should automatically appear, but if it doesn't, choose File > Import from Camera (Command-I).

2. The next step depends on the type of camera you're connecting:

   - For memory-based camcorders, click the Import All button to copy each clip's file from the device's memory or hard disk storage (**Figure 7.4**). Or, change the import setting to Manual, click which clips to import, and then click the Import Checked button.

Figure 7.4
*Importing
selected clips
in iMovie*

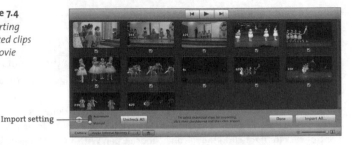

Import setting

- For a tape-based camcorder, click the Import button to start copy-ing the data on tape to the hard disk. To find individual clips, use the playback controls to start importing at the start of each clip.

3. In the next dialog, enter a name for the Event in which it will appear, and optionally choose to analyze the video for stabilization (which can significantly extend the time it takes to import). Click Import.

   After the clips import, they appear in the Event Library for editing.

4. Click Done to close the Import window.

> **tip** Obviously, I don't have room to cover iMovie in depth here, but I have a better suggestion: Buy my book! *The iMovie '11 Project Book* covers everything you want to know about making great movies in iMovie. Also see my iMovie blog (jeffcarlson.com/imovie/) for more information.

QuickTime Player

QuickTime Player has always been a general-purpose "open everything" video and audio player. For example, when you choose to download a movie trailer in HD at Apple's site (trailers.apple.com), the job is handed off to QuickTime Player.

To play a video file, download it and do the following:

1. Launch QuickTime Player.

2. Choose File > Open and select your video file, or drag the file onto the QuickTime Player icon in the Dock. The file opens in QuickTime Player.

> **tip** Since several applications can read video formats, double-clicking a file doesn't guarantee it will open in QuickTime Player. To be sure, Control-click (or right-click) the file and choose Open With > QuickTime Player.

3. Click the Play button in the playback controls or press the spacebar to begin playing (**Figure 7.5**). After a few seconds, the playback controls and the title bar disappear, leaving just the movie.

Figure 7.5
A movie in QuickTime Player, with the controller

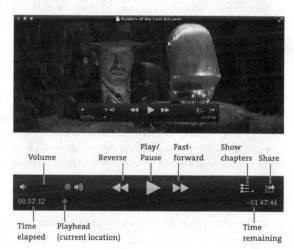

> **note** Some playback controls appear only in some circumstances. For example, the Share button is disabled when you're viewing a movie with copy protection. Also, when viewing a movie full screen, a Zoom icon appears

that toggles between watching widescreen movies in a letterboxed format and filling the screen with the image (which cuts off the left and right edges of the picture).

Stream content over the Internet

Some Web sites offer content as an on-demand stream instead of as a standalone downloaded file. Usually the site will include a link that opens QuickTime Player, but sometimes you may need (or prefer) to enter the address directly. Choose File > Open Location (Command-L) and enter the address. When playback begins, the Reverse and Fast-forward buttons are gone, leaving just Play/Pause. However, you can move the playhead to a location in the movie; QuickTime buffers the content beginning at that point instead of loading everything up to it.

Record a video or audio clip

Although iMovie and GarageBand offer features for making on-the-spot audio and video recordings, if you're putting together something quick and easy, you may want a simple utility like QuickTime Player to do the recording.

Need to send a birthday greeting to your nephew who lives on the other side of the world? Create a recording using the following steps.

1. In QuickTime Player, choose File > New Movie Recording (Command-Option-N) or File > New Audio Recording (Command-Control-Option-N). A new window appears; if you're recording video and your Mac has a camera built-in or attached, say hi to yourself.

2. In the controller area, click the pop-up menu to set the quality of the video, the input sources, and the location for the recorded movie file (**Figure 7.6**, on the next page).

Figure 7.6
Movie recording settings

3. Click the red Record button to begin recording. The video controls area displays the elapsed time and amount of disk space consumed, as well as the incoming audio levels.

   After a few seconds, the controls area disappears, replaced by a subtle indicator of the audio levels. Moving your pointer over the window makes it reappear.

4. Click the red Stop button to halt recording. The file you created is automatically saved in the directory you chose in step 2, and opens in the player.

Record your screen

Sometimes it's easier to show someone how to do something on your computer than to try to explain it over the phone. With QuickTime Player, you can record your screen.

1. Choose File > New Screen Recording (Command-Control-N). A Screen Recording controller appears.

2. Use the pop-up menu to specify settings for the recording.

   If you don't want to record the audio, which includes you speaking, make sure the Microphone option is set to None.

   To view circles where you click the mouse button, enable the Show Mouse Clicks in Recording option.

3. Click the Record button. Here you have two options: Click once to record the entire screen, or drag a selection to record just that portion of the screen. If you're recording a selection, click the Start Recording button to begin.

4. When you're finished, click the Stop Recording button or press Command-Control-Esc. The movie file opens.

tip If you anticipate needing to record your screen more often, such as for interactive tutorials, check out Telestream's ScreenFlow (www.telestream.net/screen-flow/).

Trim videos

Once you've opened or recorded a video clip, you can trim the footage. It's a fast, easy way to cut out extraneous bits of a video clip, such as the first few seconds while you were waiting for something to happen. Trimming affects just one clip—if you need to edit several clips, turn to iMovie.

1. Open a video clip you wish to trim in QuickTime Player.

2. Choose Edit > Trim (Command-T). The trimming bar appears.

3. Drag the left or right edges to remove sections of the clip (**Figure 7.7**).

Figure 7.7
Trimming a clip

Drag edge of trimmer bar.

4. Click the Trim button or press Return to apply the trim.

5. Choose File > Save As to save your edited file.

> **tip** Here's a neat feature: Choose Edit > Select All Excluding Silence. Silent portions at the start or end of the clip are assumed to be moments when you were waiting for something to happen and are set for removal when you complete the trim.

> **tip** The trimmer bar only removes frames from the beginning and end of a clip. If you have two or more portions of a longer clip you want to save, duplicate the file in the Finder, then trim each copy to the section you want.

> **note** You cannot trim movies that include copy protection, such as movies you purchase through the iTunes Store.

Share media

Don't let the video sit neglected on your hard disk—send it to a host of destinations, such as Facebook, YouTube, Vimeo, and more.

1. Click the Share button in the controller (**Figure 7.8**).

Figure 7.8
*Sharing from
the controller*

2. Choose a destination from the pop-up menu that appears.

3. Enter information about the video and share it, based on the service.

Share with AirPlay

If you own an Apple TV (second generation or later), you can use it to display what's on your Mac's screen. This feature, called mirroring, is great for giving presentations or when working in a classroom, especially since no wires are required. AirPlay mirroring happens entirely over the Wi-Fi network.

When Mountain Lion detects an Apple TV on the same network, an AirPlay Mirroring icon appears in the menu bar. Click it and select the Apple TV you wish to use for mirroring (**Figure 7.9**).

Figure 7.9
AirPlay Mirroring enabled

Some apps, like iTunes, can take advantage of AirPlay by sending video to the TV. Look for the AirPlay button in the playback controls or elsewhere in the interface and then choose the name of the Apple TV (**Figure 7.10**).

Figure 7.10
AirPlay in iTunes

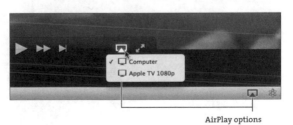

AirPlay options

Have Fun with Photo Booth

I initially thought Photo Booth was a nifty distraction, a way to highlight the fact that most Macs now include a built-in camera. The application takes a photo or video and offers effects that you can apply and ways to share the finished pic.

To take a photo, click the Take Photo button in the middle of the toolbar (and smile!). Photo Booth counts down from 3 to 1 before taking the shot. To better replicate the old photo booth machines, click the second button on the toolbar, which makes Photo Booth capture four quick shots in succession when you click the Take Photo button.

Photo Booth includes several visual effects to spice up (or completely weird out) your self-portraits. Click the Effects button in the toolbar to view the available effects; the arrows to each side of the button display more effects. Click the effect you want to use, then take your photo.

To share a photo, select it in the tray and then click one of the buttons on the toolbar to attach the photo to a new outgoing message in Mail (or your default email program), add the picture to iPhoto, use it as your user account photo, or assign it as your buddy picture in Messages. You can also drag a photo from the tray to the Desktop, a visible Finder window, or a document in another application.

8

Disks and Networking

No computer is an island, and you will frequently find yourself needing to move files from one computer to another. OS X has many options for connecting storage devices to a Mac and for connecting to other computers over a network, whether a local network or the Internet. In this chapter, I cover how to attach and remove (or *mount* and *unmount*) drives, as well as how to manage drives over a network.

To move files between computers, the AirDrop feature makes transferring files painless. You can also use the Finder to burn data to a CD or DVD, or copy files to specific locations on another computer.

Networking isn't just about copying files, however. Using Mountain Lion's screen sharing features, you can view and control someone else's screen—a great feature for troubleshooting a family member's computer remotely.

Connect a Storage Device

You'll run into two main kinds of storage devices: hard disk drives, which are enclosed in a case and attached via a cable; and memory drives (also called flash or thumb drives), which plug into a USB port.

External disk drives

Hard disk drives come in enclosures, cases that contain a power supply and interface ports along with the drive itself. (Some drives may not include cables, so double-check before you buy.) Depending on your Mac, you may be able to connect drives to your computer with FireWire 400, FireWire 800, USB 2.0, or Thunderbolt interfaces. Some Macs that are capable of running Mountain Lion, like the MacBook Air and MacBook Pro with Retina Display, lack any FireWire ports, but adapters are available.

FireWire 400 and FireWire 800 are two different speeds of the same standard, and each has a different connector type. The faster and slower versions are compatible with each other, however. Modern USB drives support USB 2.0 or 3.0, which use a standard cable that works with all computers and drives. Thunderbolt shares the same plug style as Mini DisplayPort, the connector used by modern Macs to connect external displays; in fact, Thunderbolt can be used to connect monitors and hard drives, provided you have a display or hub with Thunderbolt ports.

tip You can purchase an adapter to let a FireWire 400 drive connect to a computer that has just a FireWire 800 connector. However, it will still transfer data only at the slower speed.

Memory drives

A memory drive contains a small memory chip of the same sort used for digital camera storage. The drive has a connector, nearly always USB 2.0, that allows the drive to be used with a computer. Memory drives can be extremely tiny and can come in whimsical designs, such as molded plastic versions of popular sushi dishes or cartoon characters.

Connect a drive

With a spare port available, plug the cable between an external hard drive and the computer, and then turn on the drive's power. Although you can power up a drive before the computer cable is plugged in, it's considered generally safer to connect the cable first.

A memory drive doesn't require external power. Simply plug it into an available port and make sure it's securely inserted.

USB Hubbub

If all your USB ports are occupied, you can typically add a USB hub, which extends a single USB connection to allow two or more additional devices. Memory drives are sometimes built without enough space to allow them to be plugged into a USB port. A USB hub can give you better access, and you can locate it in a more convenient place than the back of the computer.

A *powered* USB hub is a better choice than a passive hub. A powered hub has to be plugged in separately to AC power, but it also allows the use of nearly any kind of USB device. Passive hubs, which are powered by the computer via the USB port, sometimes cannot pull enough juice to operate certain kinds of USB devices, such as cameras or even phone chargers.

Speaking of USB hubs, you may already have one: a wired keyboard, which contains USB ports. Also, many third-party monitors include USB ports, turning the monitor into a hub as well.

Work with a mounted volume

When the drive is fully powered up, an icon representing the volume appears on the Desktop and in the sidebar of Finder windows (**Figure 8.1**).

Figure 8.1
A mounted hard drive

A mounted volume appears on the Desktop and in the sidebar.

note   Generally, a volume's icon indicates the type of drive or connection it uses, but sometimes a volume may appear with a generic icon.

Mounted volumes can be used just like a hard drive inside the computer. Memory drives and external hard drives can be used in precisely the same manner, too.

tip   If you'd rather not clutter your Desktop, choose Finder > Preferences and, in the General pane, choose which items appear.

Unmount a volume

When you've finished using a volume and want to remove it from the computer, it's critical that you eject it properly via software first. The Finder provides several options:

- Select the drive and choose File > Eject or press Command-E.

- Right-click the drive and choose Eject from the contextual menu.

- Drag the drive to the Dock's Trash icon, which changes to an Eject icon.

- Click the Eject icon to the right of a volume's name in the sidebar of a Finder window.

Don't detach the cable from your computer or power down an external drive, or pull out a memory drive, until you are sure that OS X has finished several behind-the-scenes tasks for ejecting. The drive icon turns from solid to a grayed-back version while OS X completes the removal process. Only when the drive disappears from the Desktop is it safe to disconnect the drive.

 Volumes are also safely unmounted when you shut down a Mac. When the shutdown process is complete, drives can be detached.

 Another way to verify that a volume has been unmounted is to install HardwareGrowler, a component of Growl (growl.info) that displays an unobtrusive message when your hardware configuration changes.

If you've opened any files from a mounted drive, OS X won't let you eject the volume until the file is closed. Mountain Lion tells you which programs are tying up the volume (**Figure 8.2**).

Figure 8.2
Mountain Lion tells you what's preventing a volume from ejecting.

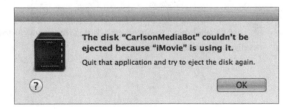

The disk "CarlsonMediaBot" couldn't be ejected because "iMovie" is using it.
Quit that application and try to eject the disk again.

OK

note If you remove a drive before Mountain Lion is finished cleaning up hidden files and settings, the drive may not be mountable. Launch Disk Utility (found in the Utilities folder within the Applications folder) and run repair on the volume to try to fix it.

Connect to a Networked Computer

If you own more than one computer or work with other people on projects, files you need are often located somewhere other than on the machine in front of you. Networked file serving, in which a computer offers up access over a network to hard drives attached to it, lets you have all the documents you need at your fingertips.

note A server can share a single folder as if it were a complete volume to limit access to the rest of the files on a drive. This is useful when working with others who don't need (or who shouldn't have) full drive access.

Mount a networked volume

Computers on the network that have shared access enabled appear in two locations in the Finder (**Figure 8.3**).

- Choose Go > Network (Command-Shift-K).

- Look in the Shared heading in the sidebar of a Finder window.

tip Computers running OS X and other operating systems show up in the list of available computers; machines running Windows and other systems display a generic PC icon.

Figure 8.3
*Networked
computers
appear in the
sidebar and the
Network window.*

Available computers —

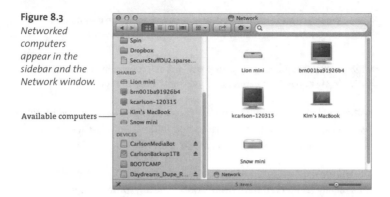

To mount a volume over the network, you must first connect to the
server, then select the volume.

1. Double-click the computer's icon in the Network window, or select it
   from the Shared heading in the sidebar.

2. The window changes to show a connection in progress. The upper left
   displays "Connecting" until a connection is made. If a Guest account is
   set up on the computer you're connecting to, OS X shows any folders
   available to guest users (**Figure 8.4**). If this is all you need, skip to step 4.

Figure 8.4
*Connected to
another Mac
as Guest*

3. Click the Connect As button at the upper right. Enter the user name
   and password for the computer to which you are connecting.

note When you store a password, anyone using the same user account on the computer can mount the server without a password.

tip In the dialog asking for your password, select Remember This Password in My Keychain to bypass step 3 the next time you connect.

4. After you log in, the Finder window displays a list of available volumes, which can include both hard drives and folders. Double-click any volume to mount it on your computer.

Mounted network volumes appear on the Desktop and in the sidebar, just as locally connected hard drives do. However, some routine operations, like opening and saving large files, will be slow if your network isn't set up using gigabit Ethernet connections.

tip Want an easier way to mount a network volume? Select it on the Desktop and choose File > Make Alias (Command-L). The next time you want to mount that volume, simply double-click the alias. If you haven't saved the password, you are prompted to enter it again.

Unmount a network volume

Unmount network volumes in the same way as you would a local drive.

- Select the drive and choose File > Eject or press Command-E.

- Right-click the drive and choose Eject from the contextual menu.

- Drag the drive to the Dock's Trash icon, which changes to an Eject icon.

- Click the Eject icon to the right of a computer's name in the sidebar of a Finder window; this option ejects *all* of the computer's mounted volumes.

View and Control a Network Computer's Screen

In Chapter 6, I demonstrated how to use Messages to share someone's screen. You can do the same thing with another Mac on your network without involving Messages.

1. In the Finder, connect to a network server and click the Share Screen button at the top of the window.

2. Enter your user name and password. The other screen appears in a window on your computer (**Figure 8.5**). When the pointer is within that window, you can control the computer remotely. Close the Screen Sharing window when you're done.

Figure 8.5
Controlling a networked computer using screen sharing

Shared screen ——

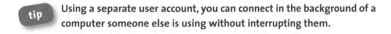
Using a separate user account, you can connect in the background of a computer someone else is using without interrupting them.

tip I use Stefan Klieme's ScreenSharingMenulet to quickly share screens of Macs on my network from the menu bar. Find it at www.klieme.com/ScreenSharingMenulet.html.

Back to My Mac

Back to My Mac lets you access computers you control beyond the local network you're on, just as if they appeared on the local network. This magic is carried out by using iCloud to provide a kind of network glue.

On each computer for which you want remote access enabled, open the iCloud preference pane and enter your iCloud user name and password. Click the Back to My Mac button and click Start to activate the service.

Computers reachable via Back to My Mac appear just like any other computer on your local network. You can connect to their files and also share their screens. However, network performance is restricted to the slower of the two connections.

Share Files from Your Mac

So far, this chapter has focused on connecting *to* another computer. But what if yours is the "other" computer? Or, what if you just want to transfer a few files? Mountain Lion provides a few simple ways to share files with other people, whether they're using OS X, Windows, or other operating systems.

Send files using AirDrop

AirDrop finds nearby computers and lets you exchange files between them with drag-and-drop simplicity. There's no need to establish an authenticated connection between machines, as described elsewhere in this chapter. AirDrop has a catch, though: You need a recent Mac that supports the feature. (My 2008 Mac mini, for example, doesn't have the hardware for AirDrop, which relies on a processor component.) To share files using AirDrop, do the following:

1. Click the AirDrop button in the sidebar on each computer. Your Mac appears at the bottom of the window, and other AirDrop-capable computers show up as circles around it.

2. Drag one or more files or folders to a computer's icon (**Figure 8.6**).

Figure 8.6
Sending a file using AirDrop

3. When OS X asks if you'd like to transfer the file, click the Send button (**Figure 8.7**).

Figure 8.7
Confirm that you want to send the file to that computer.

4. The person on the other computer confirms that they want to receive the file by clicking either Save or Save and Open (which opens it using the default application for that file type). The files appear in the Downloads folder.

Dropbox for File Synchronization

Copying files between computers via a network is useful when you need just a few files. However, you may want the same sets of files everywhere you work. Dropbox (www.dropbox.com) automatically synchronizes the contents of a folder at two or more locations. Dropbox preserves older versions of files, and acts as an offsite backup as well. (I made extensive use of Dropbox while writing this book, automatically sharing screenshots from Mountain Lion test machines to my main computer.)

Dropbox also lets you share the contents of specific folders with other people and vice versa, allowing you to have the same set of files as project collaborators or family members. Another option is to create photo galleries from photos placed in folders.

You install a small software program that constantly monitors for changes in a folder (with as many nested folders as you want) on your computer, and receives notification of changes on other machines.

The service requires that you set up an account, which comes with 2 GB of storage at no cost. You can pay for more storage: 50 GB is $9.99 a month or $99 a year; 100 GB is $19.99 a month or $199 a year.

Enable file sharing

AirDrop is convenient and easy to use but doesn't offer much control. When you need more access to a computer, such as the ability to copy files to a specific folder, use OS X's file sharing features. Perform the following steps to share files.

1. Open the Sharing preference pane (**Figure 8.8**).

2. Name your computer in the Computer Name field. (By default, OS X inserts "*Your Name*'s Computer".)

3. Select the File Sharing checkbox in the Service menu at left to enable sharing.

Figure 8.8
The Sharing preference pane

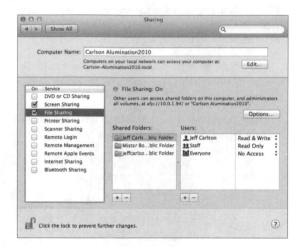

Choose one or more file sharing methods

Mountain Lion uses two standard file sharing methods. Click the Options button to enable or disable the following:

- **AFP (Apple Filing Protocol).** AFP works with OS X (and earlier Mac OS) systems. It's rarely used except among Macs and certain networked hard drives. That said, AFP is enabled by default. If you're connecting only to Macs, you don't need to do anything else.

- **SMB (sometimes called Samba).** The Windows default method for many years, SMB is also commonly used by other operating systems.

Specify what to share

You have complete control over which items are shared from the computer. Changes are applied immediately.

note You're not limited to sharing folders, even though the field is called **Shared Folders**. Hard disks and memory drives can also be shared to users with administrator privileges.

- To add items to share, click the Add (+) button beneath the Shared Folders field. You can also drag a folder or drive from the Finder into the area.

  Shared items, and all nested folders within them, display a banner across the top of any Finder window (**Figure 8.9**).

Figure 8.9
A shared folder in the Finder

- To remove shared items, select the item and click the Remove (–) button.

Set who gets access

Mountain Lion lets you control who may access a given shared folder or drive, and what privileges they have to make changes or view the contents.

With an item selected in the Shared Folders list, those who have permission appear in the Users list at right. Each entry is either a user with an account on the computer or a group of users. Two special groups also appear:

- **Everyone**, which is any user on the system, including the Guest user.

- **Administrators**, which includes any user who has the administrative option set for installing software or making other system configuration changes.

Guest Access

There's a dangerous combination of file sharing and guest access that you may need to guard against. In the Users & Groups preference pane, the Guest User account is used to let people log in to OS X without having privileged access and without leaving a trace (see Chapter 2).

However, it's also used to provide anonymous, password-free access to shared volumes that are marked as available to everyone. Guest access to shared folders is enabled by default.

Because AFP file sharing works over the Internet, if your Mac is directly connected using a publicly available address and guest access is available, anything in the Public folder of any account on the machine is available, even if you'd intended it just for yourself or other users on a local network.

I recommend disabling guest access to folders:

1. In the Users & Groups preference pane, click the lock icon and enter an administrative account and password to make changes.

2. Select the Guest User account.

3. Deselect the option "Allow guests to connect to shared folders."

Add users

If you're the only person who will access your Mac from another machine, your user account and privileges are already set up. Simply use your regular user name and password to gain access to your files.

You can also add users to a folder or drive by clicking the Add (+) button below the Users field, then choosing one of three methods (**Figure 8.10**):

Figure 8.10
Choose users who need access to a shared volume.

- Select the Users & Groups list item, choose a user or group in the right-hand pane, and click Select. These are users and groups that have already been created on the computer. Any users or groups already assigned to a shared item are grayed out.

- Click the Contacts item, select a person from your contacts, and click Select. Doing so creates a sharing-only user account, which may only remotely log in to the computer to access files, and which may not log in from the computer itself.

- Click New Person and type a user name in the New Person dialog. Enter a password and verify it, then click Create Account. Select the person's name from the Users & Groups list and click Select to add them to the Users list.

note Even if you remove a user from the Sharing preference pane, the account still exists in the Users & Groups preference pane; go there if you want to delete the user from the computer entirely (see Chapter 2).

Choose what actions users and groups may perform

Each user or group may have one of three settings applied (**Figure 8.11**):

Figure 8.11
Each user or group may have separate permissions set for access.

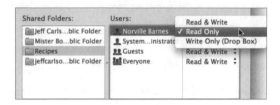

- **Read & Write.** This is the most common option, and allows the user or group to add, modify, or delete any item within the shared item.

- **Read Only.** This option limits the user or group to viewing a list of files and folders, and viewing the contents of any files. New files or folders may not be added, no changes may be made, and no item may be deleted.

- **Write Only (Drop Box).** If you need to allow someone to copy files to you, but not see anything else contained in a shared volume, this option lets them add items to a folder without seeing the contents of the folder.

A fourth option, No Access, is available only for the special Everyone group. You might want some users on a system to have access, but not every user.

 Changes made to file-sharing privileges also affect the rights of user accounts on the same machine when they're logged in.

tip OS X can share files even when the computer is asleep. In the Energy Saver preference pane, select the "Wake for network access" option. The computer still appears in the sidebar of Finder windows and the Network window, so other machines can connect to it. When that happens, the computer wakes up. This applies to sharing iTunes libraries, too, not just files.

Burn a CD or DVD

You don't have to mount a drive directly or over a network to share files. OS X also supports the capability to write, or *burn*, them to a CD or DVD.

1. In the Finder, select items you want to burn. You can choose a folder, files, or any combination—even a mounted drive—as long as the contents will be able to fit on a single CD or DVD.

2. Choose File > Burn *[name* or *number of items]* to Disc.

3. Mountain Lion prompts you to insert a blank CD or DVD. The dialog box states how much storage is needed. Insert the disc.

4. Name the disc and, optionally, choose the speed at which it is burned (**Figure 8.12**).

Figure 8.12
Name the disc and choose a speed.

Are you sure you want to burn the contents of
"iPad_for_Photogs.fpbf" to a disc?

You can use this disc on any Mac or Windows computer. To eject the disc without burning it, click Eject.

Disc Name: iPad_for_Photogs

Burn Speed: Maximum Possible (24x)

☐ Save Burn Folder To: iPad_for_Photogs

Eject   Cancel   Burn

5. Click Burn. OS X burns the disc and then verifies it. When the process is complete, the disc appears on the desktop as a mounted volume.

tip Most modern optical drives can burn at the maximum rate. If you've had problems with disc burning failures, choose a slower rate, which is less likely to produce errors.

9

Back Up Your Data

I considered titling this chapter "MAKE BACKUPS!!" but didn't want to give my copyeditor a heart attack. Even without the all-caps and double exclamation points, I can't overstress the importance of setting up a good backup system.

If you think backups are merely a fine idea, and maybe you plan to copy a file or two to a CD once in awhile, let me propose this situation: You're sitting in front of your Mac, looking through your digital photos of when your kids were babies, or when you took that once-in-a-lifetime vacation. Then you start to hear a clicking noise, followed by your computer abruptly shutting down. When you restart it, the clicking noise has returned but nothing else.

Congratulations! Your hard disk has just suffered a head crash.

The mechanism that reads the data has broken and started chopping into the disk surface—that clicking sound—destroying any chance of restoring your data. Without a backup, your only hope is to pay a thousand bucks to have a company such as DriveSavers (drivesaversdatarecovery.com) extract the data in a dust-free environment using forensic tools.

I'm not exaggerating. Disk failures have happened to me—a few times. Hard disks fail, optical media degrades, disk directories become corrupted, laptops are stolen or are damaged. And your digital photos and other information are gone forever. The question is: What will you do to ensure your data remains safe?

Backups, backups, backups!

The Pieces of a Good Backup System

Now that I've sufficiently scared you, I'm happy to point out that a good backup system is entirely possible. OS X includes Time Machine, a feature that automatically backs up your data every hour to an external hard drive or a network volume (including Apple's Time Capsule).

Notice I said "a good backup *system*." If your Mac's hard drive fails, you'll have the Time Machine backup, but what if that fails, too? To do this right (and you do want to do it right), a backup system needs a few key components:

- **An automatic backup.** The backup should happen with as little inter- vention from you as possible, to ensure that it gets done. Unless you're obsessively organized, it's easy to forget to connect a disk or run backup software on a regular schedule. Time Machine is one of the best features in OS X, because it backs up your data in the background every hour.

- **A versioned backup.** Time Machine stores multiple copies of a file as it existed over time, so, for example, you can go back and retrieve the first draft of a document.

- **A bootable duplicate.** People focus on loss of data when something catastrophic happens, but don't forget about the loss of time. If your hard disk dies, you want to get up and running again without delay. In addition to a Time Machine backup, you want a recent complete duplicate of your hard disk that can be used to start up the computer (connected via FireWire, USB, or Thunderbolt).

- **An offsite backup.** You can have multiple backups of your computer, but if a fire destroys your house, it will likely destroy all the copies of your data, too. Make sure your data is also backed up to another location, whether that involves copying important files to Dropbox or another Internet-based backup system, or taking a duplicate hard drive to your office, a trusted friend's house, or a bank safe-deposit box.

- **On-the-spot backups.** In addition to the elements above, you'll probably have smaller, temporary backups for important files that you're working on. Those could be stored online or on CDs or DVDs, keychain memory drives, or another source.

My backup system

I know. It sounds daunting and complicated. But I'm no longer willing to risk the loss of my data, and I hope you feel the same way. If you don't want to be this comprehensive, or the cost is too great, at the very least use Time Machine on an external hard disk.

To give you an idea of what this looks like in a real-world setting, **Figure 9.1** (on the next page) illustrates my current backup system.

Figure 9.1
A diagram of my personal backup system

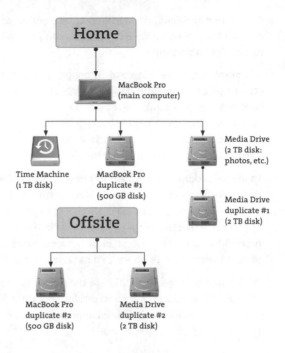

The duplicate drives stored offsite and at home are rotated every few weeks, so I always have a recent duplicate at home and away.

note

note

I've built my system based on the recommendations of my friend and colleague Joe Kissell, who's written extensively about the subject. I recommend his book *Take Control of Backing Up Your Mac* (I edited several editions). (www.takecontrolbooks.com/backing-up).

Time Machine

Mountain Lion's Time Machine feature automatically performs a versioned backup of your entire hard disk, and updates it once every hour. If something happens—whether your Mac's hard drive dies or you accidentally delete a file—Time Machine can retrieve the data from the backup.

Set up Time Machine

Time Machine is enabled by default, making it easy to get started.

1. Connect an external hard disk to your computer. If this is the first time the disk has been mounted, a dialog appears asking if you'd like to use it as a Time Machine backup.

2. Select the Encrypt Backup Disk option if you want to secure the data in the event someone tries to access it normally (if it were stolen, for example).

3. Click Use as Backup Disk to press the disk into service. The Time Machine preference pane opens and the first backup begins. If you click Don't Use, Time Machine ignores that drive as a backup source in the future (you can manually choose to use it later).

To manually specify a disk to use for the backup, open the Time Machine system preferences, click the Select Disk button, choose one, and click Use Disk (**Figure 9.2**).

Figure 9.2
*Choosing a
backup disk*

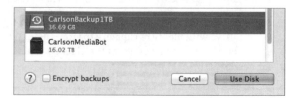

note The first backup could take quite a long time, depending on how much data is on your computer. Although you can still use your Mac while Time Machine is working, the initial backup may slow your system a bit. Start the process at night and let the copying happen while you sleep.

note You can use one external drive to back up multiple computers using Time Machine (provided you're willing to cart the drive to each machine). Each Mac gets its own directory on the backup disk. Just be sure to have plenty of free space to handle the needs of all the computers.

note It's also possible to use a network volume as a Time Machine backup. Mount the disk in the Finder (see Chapter 8 for more details), and set it as the backup disk in the Time Machine preference pane. You need to make sure the volume is mounted for ongoing backups.

How Much Storage for Time Machine?

When looking to buy an external hard disk, I recommend that you purchase the highest-capacity drive you can afford—at least 500 GB, but 1 TB or more is better.

When Time Machine makes a copy of a file that has changed, it holds onto the existing copy it made during the last backup. This approach is what enables you to reach back in time and grab the version from last Wednesday if you need it. Time Machine preserves hourly backups of files changed within the last 24 hours; daily backups for the past month; and weekly backups for all previous months.

All those copies take up space on the Time Machine disk, so you want a drive with plenty of capacity to store them. When the disk does fill up, Time Machine deletes the oldest backups to make room for new files.

Exclude items from the backup

You may not want to back up everything on your computer using Time Machine. For example, if you use virtualization software to run Windows, the data is stored in a multi-gigabyte disk image. Making one change to that environment flags the entire disk image as being modified, so Time Machine makes a new copy the next time it runs.

1. Open the Time Machine preferences.

2. Click the Options button.

3. Click the Add (+) button and choose the disk, folder, or file you wish to exclude (**Figure 9.3**); or, simply drag the item from the Finder to the dialog.

4. Click Save to exit the dialog.

Figure 9.3
Exclude items from the backup.

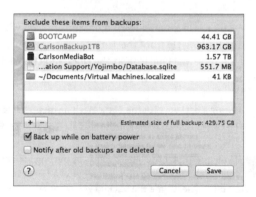

If you do exclude things from a Time Machine backup, make sure **note** they're being backed up using some other method. You don't want to be reminded that you omitted something later when you need to get it back.

Perform a backup manually

Time Machine backs up files every hour, so there's no need to schedule a backup time. However, you may wish to manually trigger a backup, such as when you've finished a project or before upgrading software. To do so, go to the Time Machine icon in the menu bar and choose Back Up Now. (If you don't see the Time Machine icon, open the Time Machine preference pane and ensure that the "Show Time Machine in menu bar" option is selected.)

> **tip** If you do want to gain more control over when Time Machine backs up data, install TimeMachineScheduler, which lets you set an interval for the backup to occur and can skip a time range—forcing Time Machine to operate only at night, for example (www.klieme.com/TimeMachineScheduler.html).

Pause a backup

If Time Machine is in the middle of a backup and you want to cancel it, choose Stop Backing Up from the Time Machine menu bar menu; or, click and hold the Time Machine icon in the Dock and choose the same thing. The next scheduled backup will occur on time.

> **tip** During a backup, click the Time Machine menu bar icon to view the backup's progress (such as "Backing Up: 1.35 GB of 6.92 GB").

> **tip** If you interrupt a backup—such as by putting your computer to sleep or ejecting the backup disk—don't worry. Time Machine will pick up where it left off the next time the backup volume is available.

Restore files from a backup

On a few occasions, Time Machine has saved my bacon by recovering files I'd accidentally deleted. Here's how to locate and restore old files.

1. In the Finder, do one of the following:

   ■ Open a window containing the folder where your desired file should appear.

   ■ Type the name of the file (or other search criteria) in the Search field of a Finder window.

2. Click the Time Machine icon in the Dock, or choose Enter Time Machine from the Time Machine menu in the menu bar. Everything but the Finder window is replaced by a starry interface, and your mind is blown (**Figure 9.4**).

Figure 9.4
Time Machine activated

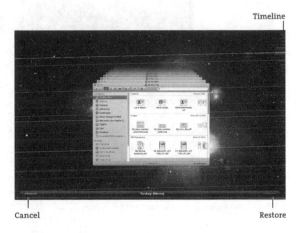

Timeline

Cancel   Restore

You can also browse your hard disk in this Finder window if you choose not to use the Search field.

3. Click the top arrow to the right of the window to jump back to the most recent stored copy of the file (**Figure 9.5**, on the next page). If you need an earlier version, click the arrow again until you've located the one you want.

Figure 9.5
Locating a deleted file

Back/forward in time

 tip Select a file and press the spacebar to activate Quick Look on any file to make sure you're getting the right one.

4. Select the file and click the Restore button. The file is copied from the backup drive to its original location, and you're returned to the Finder.

tip Although the backup volume is mounted right there on your desktop, don't go poking through it to find a file—you're much better off letting Time Machine do the locating for you.

Restore an entire drive

In the event that something catastrophic happens (most likely a hard drive failure) and you need to recover your entire drive's worth of data, you can do it from the Time Machine backup.

1. Start your computer from the Mountain Lion Recovery HD: Restart the Mac and hold Command-R. (Or, hold the Option key, and then choose the Recovery drive from the list of startup disks.)

2. Select the Restore From Time Machine Backup option in the OS X Utilities window, and click Continue.

3. After reading the warning that restoring erases everything currently on your disk, click Continue and then select your Time Machine drive.

4. Select one of the full Time Machine backups listed in the next window.

5. Select the destination disk (your Mac's internal hard disk, most likely), and click the Restore button.

tip If your original data was destroyed, you probably want the most recent full backup. However, if your Mac became unstable after installing some software, or you think some other event could have corrupted the data, choose an earlier backup from the list.

Consider a Time Capsule

If you use a laptop or have several Macs in your house, it may not be convenient to attach an external hard drive to each one. (My wife's MacBook stays in the living room, and she doesn't want a hard drive and its associated cables as table decoration.) Apple's Time Capsule device is a wireless AirPort base station with a built-in hard disk set up to use Time Machine (www.apple.com/timecapsule/).

Once the Time Capsule is set up, you can choose it as a backup disk in the Time Machine preference pane. Copying files over a wireless network is slower than copying to an attached hard disk, so for the first backup, connect the Mac and Time Machine via Ethernet.

The Time Capsule also features the ability to make an archive of its contents, giving you a backup of your backup. Use AirPort Utility (located in the Utilities folder) to create an archive.

Make a Duplicate

Having a duplicate of your hard disk means you can get your computer running again quickly. However, making a duplicate is more involved than merely copying your files from one disk to another in the Finder (an approach that worked in the Mac OS 9 days). OS X hides many system files from view, so the best action to take is to use a duplication program such as SuperDuper (www.shirt-pocket.com) or Carbon Copy Cloner (www.bombich.com). Both applications copy everything and set up the external disk so that you can start up your computer from it.

Make a duplicate using SuperDuper

SuperDuper and Carbon Copy Cloner operate similarly, but I'm going to go through the steps of setting up a duplicate in SuperDuper, since that's what I currently use.

1. Attach and mount an external hard disk.

2. Launch SuperDuper.

> **tip** SuperDuper can erase the backup drive during its progress, so you don't need to format it beforehand.

3. Choose your Mac's hard disk from the Copy pop-up menu, then choose the backup drive from the "to" pop-up menu (**Figure 9.6**).

4. Choose Backup - all files from the "using" pop-up menu. SuperDuper provides other options, such as copying only changed files, but for this example you want to make a complete duplicate of the drive.

5. Click Copy Now to start the process. Enter your administrator password and then click the Copy button in the dialog confirming your action. The backup commences.

Figure 9.6
SuperDuper

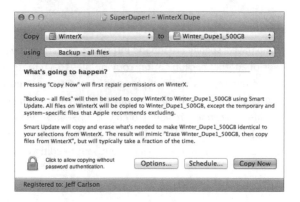

The Amazing Hard Disk Toaster

With all my talk of backing up to external hard disks and making duplicates, you're probably envisioning a nightmare of cables and power adapters. That doesn't have to be the case.

Instead of buying external drives that include an enclosure, ports, and an always-bulky power supply, I bought a "toaster": one device into which you insert bare SATA hard drives. The one I purchased, a NewerTech Voyager Q (www.newertech.com/products/voyagerq.php), sports an array of ports to connect to the computer: two FireWire 800, one FireWire 400, one USB 3.0/2.0, and one eSATA. When you insert either a 3.5-inch or 2.5-inch hard drive (just the drive itself) and power the device, the disk mounts on your desktop.

It's not something you'd want to use as a permanent disk solution, since the electronics on the bottom of the hard drive are exposed, but it's great for duplicates. Better yet, the bare drives are much less expensive than drives that come in enclosures and are easy to transport offsite; consider buying a few anti-static protective cases, such as those sold by WiebeTech (www.wiebetech.com/products/cases.php).

Back Up Files Online

If you have a speedy broadband Internet connection, you can take advantage of another backup option: copying files to a remote server. Depending on the service, files are encrypted and stored on a computer outside your house (and most likely outside your state). When you need to recover a lost file, you connect to your stored backup—either via the Web or using backup software—and copy the file back to your computer. Online backups let you maintain an offsite backup without needing to rotate drives.

Automated backups

A growing number of companies offer online backup services at various rates. I recommend CrashPlan (www.crashplan.com), which offers a CrashPlan+ plan that stores 10 GB for $1.50 a month (you can also pay for unlimited storage starting at $3 a month, or choose a family plan starting at $6 a month). CrashPlan also has a clever free option: Copy an unlimited amount of data to a friend's computer or another computer you own (such as one at work, also running CrashPlan).

However, Internet speeds are still far too slow (especially in the United States) to back up an entire hard disk—it could take weeks. The best approach is to choose which data you wish to copy offsite and continue to rely on alternate backup solutions.

note   When determining if you want to use an online backup service, keep in mind that the upstream bandwidth on your Internet service is probably far slower than what you enjoy downstream. My cable Internet service is advertised as having up to 15 Mbps (megabits per second) downstream but only 3 Mbps upstream (which itself is more than many packages).

Back up essential files

An automated backup is great for peace of mind, but I often sleep better at night after making online copies of current projects. I've started putting active projects directly into my Dropbox folder (see the sidebar "Dropbox for File Synchronization" in Chapter 8), guaranteeing that I have an offsite backup without having to do anything extra. The files are copied as soon as they're saved, and Dropbox keeps an archive of versions.

Access Previous Versions of Files

I've been using a computer long enough that I instinctively press Command-S several times while I'm working to save the document I'm working on. But what if I changed something and want to go back to an earlier version? For applications that support it, the Versions feature makes those previous incarnations easily available.

Mountain Lion's Auto Save feature automatically saves changes while you work and when you close a document. Look for an indicator in the document's title bar to reveal the current state of the file (**Figure 9.7**). At any time, you can manually save a version by choosing File > Save or pressing Command-S.

Figure 9.7
This TextEdit document has been edited since the last version was saved.

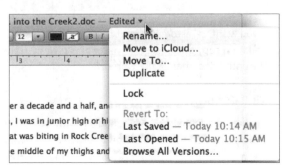

Restore a version

If you discover you want to go back to a previous version, two options are available from the pop-up menu in the document's title bar:

- Choose Revert to Last Saved Version (or Revert to Last Opened Version, if the last save was made by closing the file).

- Choose Browse All Versions. The document appears in a Time Machine-style starfield with the current version at left and saved versions at right (**Figure 9.8**).

    To bring up past versions, use the time slider at the right edge of the screen or click the title bar of the versions that recede into the past. Then, click the Restore button.

Figure 9.8
Comparing versions of a document

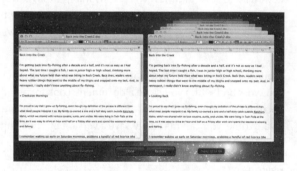

- If you want to restore just part of a file, Choose Browse All Versions and then copy and paste the material you want, rather than restore the entire document. Click Done when you're finished.

Lock a document

To ensure that a document isn't inadvertently edited, lock it by choosing Lock from the pop-up menu. If you then attempt to make a change, a dialog asks if you want to unlock the file or make a duplicate and work on that.

10

Keep Your Mac Secure

Apple made smart decisions from the first release of OS X to prevent a host of security problems from affecting its operating system. No computer is completely immune to problems such as viruses and attacks, but Mountain Lion is pretty solid.

However, that doesn't mean your data is completely safe. Miscreants who want to compromise your computer for their own purposes, steal your information to impersonate you digitally, or simply mess up your machine are always inventing new ways to break in.

To ensure the safety of your data and your use of the Internet, this chapter explains how to take full advantage of Mountain Lion's security features.

Passwords

Passwords are the unfortunate backbone of security. Unfortunate because your ability to protect something, such as access to your computer and its files, is limited by how well you choose a password.

tip If you ever receive email or a phone call that purports to be from a firm you deal with and in which someone asks for your password, it's nearly guaranteed to be a scam. If they're legitimate, there will be some mechanism for you to reset your password without divulging any sensitive information. *Never give out your password.*

Choose a strong password

Good passwords share the following traits:

- Are a mix of letters, numbers, and punctuation.

- Contain no words found in dictionaries in common languages.

- Do not substitute 3 for e, o (zero) for the letter o, or ! for the numeral 1. (These common substitutions are trivial to overcome for crackers.)

- Omit names, especially family names (that includes pet names!).

- Avoid numbers associated with your or family members' birthdays.

- Are not repeated. Use a different password for everything. (Don't worry, you won't need to memorize them all. Keep reading.)

Fortunately, Apple offers built-in help to create a strong password.

Create a password using Password Assistant

Mountain Lion includes a password generator that can create passwords for you that are as strong as you like. However, it's a little hard to find.

1. Launch the Keychain Access application, located in the Utilities folder (which is in the Applications folder).

2. Select File > New Password Item.

3. In the dialog that appears, click the key icon (🔑) to the right of the Password field. The Password Assistant appears with a password in the Suggestion field (**Figure 10.1**).

Figure 10.1
The Password Assistant helps you create strong passwords.

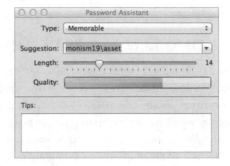

4. Choose a type of password to be generated from the Type pop-up menu, such as Memorable, which includes words in your language. If a so-called memorable password is long enough, Password Assistant includes enough other characters to make the password secure.

   You can also type your own password into the Suggestion field.

5. Click the Suggestion field's pop-up menu to see more choices. You can also drag the Length slider to change the number of characters in the password, thereby increasing its strength.

   The assistant shows how good or poor a password is through the Quality bar. Weak passwords score a short bar in red. Good passwords earn a longer bar in green.

Password Assistant is also available in other places, including the Users & Groups preference pane when creating new accounts.

 Always create the strongest password you can tolerate for user accounts in OS X. With a user account's password in hand, anyone who can walk up to your computer, connect over a local network (such as at a Wi-Fi hot spot), or reach you remotely over the Internet can access files or worse on your computer.

Store Secure Data in Your Keychain

Your sensitive data shouldn't be left out for all to see. This includes passwords, but it also includes notes to yourself that contain your credit card number or other private information you may want to access. OS X stores passwords and other security items, such as digital certificates, in keychains, which Mountain Lion encrypts using your account password as the key. Whenever you're prompted by a program or service to store a password in the keychain, a new entry is added or an existing one is modified.

note To change passwords associated with programs or services (such as AirPort Utility or Screen Sharing), don't make the changes within Keychain Access. Instead use the program in which the password was created.

Save Web site passwords

Just as you don't want to expose your private information, you also don't want to use the same password for every Web site that requires login information (such as your bank and online stores). Safari and many other Web browsers store that information in the keychain. Do the following when signing in to a secure Web site for the first time—I'm using Safari as the example browser here.

1. Load a Web site with a login form.

2. Enter your name and password, and press Return or click the Log In
   button (the name of the button varies; it's whatever sends the data).

   Safari asks if you'd like to save the password for use later (**Figure 10.2**).

Figure 10.2
*Save a Web
site password.*

3. Click Yes to save the information. If you'd prefer to always enter the
   password manually, click Never for this Website. Or, click Not Now to
   decide later. The password information is saved in the keychain and
   the Web site continues to load.

> **note** Firefox stores passwords for Web sites in its own database, not in an
> OS X keychain. You can access them in Firefox's preferences on the
> Security pane; click the Saved Passwords button.

The next time you visit that site, Safari automatically fills in the user
name and password fields; the password characters are exchanged for
bullet characters to hide the contents from peering eyes. You can log in
without looking up the information.

> **tip** If you change your mind later, it's easy to remove the saved password
> from Safari and Keychain Access. Open Safari's preferences and click
> the Passwords button. Locate a site in the list (or use the search field to find it),
> select it, and then click the Remove button.

Look up passwords in your keychain

The problem with having multiple passwords, of course, is that it's difficult to remember them all, especially ones that were generated by the Password Assistant. As long as you remember your OS X user account password, you can look up the others.

1. Launch Keychain Access and select the "login" keychain at left.

2. Locate the login you're looking for in the main list; you may want to type part of the site's name into the search field in the toolbar.

3. Double-click the login to view details about it.

4. By default, the password is not shown; click the "Show password" checkbox and enter your user account password to make it visible (**Figure 10.3**).

Figure 10.3
*View a password
in the keychain.*

(Big surprise: not
my real login
or password.)

Create secure notes

Keychain Access manages items in the keychain, which lets you view passwords you've stored and create secure notes that require your password to decrypt. Do the following to create a secure note:

1. Launch Keychain Access.

2. Select File > New Secure Note Item.

3. Enter a title and text for your note, and then click Add (**Figure 10.4**). The note is now stored securely, requiring your user account password to view it.

Figure 10.4
Create a secure note.

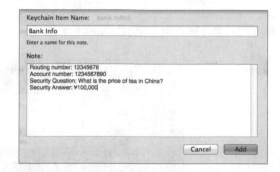

To access the contents, follow these steps:

1. In Keychain Access, double-click the secure note.

2. Select the Show Note box.

3. Enter your user account password (**Figure 10.5**). Click Always Allow to bypass entering the password again for this item. Click Allow to show the note just this one time.

Figure 10.5
Retrieve the contents of a secure note.

Essential Mountain Lion Utility: 1Password

Although OS X includes built-in methods of storing passwords and other important data, for personal information I rely on 1Password by Agile Bits (1password.com, $34.99) (**Figure 10.6**).

Figure 10.6
1Password

It can auto-fill forms using a toolbar or menu item in Firefox, Safari, Chrome, and other Web browsers (**Figure 10.7**). It also stores secure notes, and it can synchronize among your computers and with versions for the iPhone or iPod touch.

Figure 10.7
1Password Safari extension

Encrypt Your Data with FileVault

In versions of OS X prior to 10.7 Lion, I actively discouraged people from using FileVault, because it had too many limitations. Now, FileVault is a completely different beast, encrypting and decrypting the entire contents of your hard disk as needed. If your computer is stolen, the data is useless without your authorization.

Enable FileVault

To encrypt the contents of your hard disk, do the following:

1. Open the Security & Privacy preference pane and click the FileVault button.

2. Click the Turn On FileVault button. (You may need to first click the padlock button in the lower-left corner of the window to be able to make changes to the settings.)

3. If you have more than one user account, click the Enable User button and enter the passwords of each account to ensure that they can access the Mac after it's encrypted (**Figure 10.8**).

Figure 10.8
*Enable users
before encryption.*

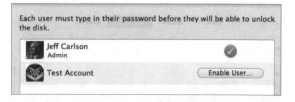

If you don't have those passwords, don't worry—you can still enter them later, but only after encryption has finished. See the note that follows these steps on the next page.

4. On the dialog that appears, write down the recovery key and store it somewhere safe (**Figure 10.9**). If you forget your password, this code can grant access to the system. Click the Continue button.

Figure 10.9
FileVault
recovery key

5. Choose whether to store the recovery key with Apple or not. Doing so requires that you choose three questions and provide answers; if you lose your recovery key, answering the questions exactly can get it back. Click Continue to proceed.

6. In the next dialog, click the Restart button to restart the Mac and begin the encryption process. While OS X is crunching the data, you can still use your computer; return to the Security & Privacy preference pane to view the progress.

Once your data is encrypted (which will take several hours), the only difference you should notice is the need to log in to your account each time you start up the computer. Files are encrypted and decrypted automatically as you work.

note You need an administrator password to enable FileVault, which can lead to an interesting situation for standard user accounts on the same machine. After the disk is encrypted, only the administrator can log in to the Mac after a restart. To authorize other users to log in, go to the Security & Privacy preference pane, click FileVault, and click the Enable Users button. Then, click the Enable User button for the account you wish to grant access for and type that account's password. The next time you restart the Mac, that account will be able to log in directly.

tip If you want to protect just some data, versus encrypting your entire hard disk, create an encrypted disk image using Apple's Disk Utility and store confidential or private files there. (Follow this link for instructions: http://db.tidbits.com/article/9673.)

General Security Precautions

Quickly increase your security through a couple of simple steps.

- **Apply security updates.** Apple's updates under Mountain Lion are installed automatically via Software Update. (If you prefer manual control, go to the Software Update preference pane and deselect the "Install system data files and security updates" option.) But this advice also counts for updates for programs you routinely use. Most software automatically notifies you of updates.

- **Turn on "Require password after sleep or screen saver begins,"** also in the Security & Privacy preference pane. This prevents easy access to your machine if left alone or behind and is especially recommended for laptops.

Enable the Firewall

Software developers stole the term *firewall* from the building industry, where construction techniques prevent a fire from passing from one compartment to another. A computer firewall keeps the bad stuff out, separating your computer from the network it's on or from the Internet.

OS X includes a modest firewall that's part of a good strategy for protecting your computer from outside influences. Firewall settings are found in the Security & Privacy preference pane in the Firewall tab.

note Apple's firewall covers incoming connections to applications only, and only in a limited fashion. More full-featured firewalls and application monitors can monitor incoming requests to services and programs, restrict those requests by address or type, and even let you know when programs are trying to reach out to the Internet. Check out DoorStop X Firewall (www.opendoor.com/DoorStop/) and Little Snitch (www.obdev.at/products/littlesnitch/).

Activate the firewall

The firewall in Mountain Lion is simple, displaying just a Start button that, when pressed, enables the feature.

1. Open the Security & Privacy preference pane and click the Firewall button. (If the Start button is grayed out, click the lock icon and provide your user account password.)

2. Click Start to activate the firewall.

Control access to applications

With the firewall turned on, you'll be asked when launching an application whether you want to allow it to accept incoming connections; for instance, iPhoto with library sharing enabled lets others browse pictures over the network. Click Allow to give it the all-clear approval (**Figure 10.10**).

Figure 10.10
The firewall doing its job

For a few more options, click the Advanced button (**Figure 10.11**).

Figure 10.11
*Set advanced
options for
the firewall.*

Choose to allow or
block connections
to a given program.

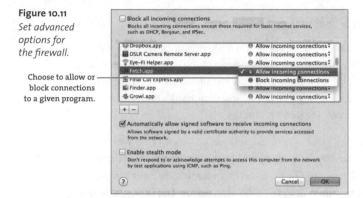

- **Block all incoming connections.** This option prevents any inbound access except for a few limited services, including Back to My Mac.

- **Individual service settings.** Each service that allows incoming access appears in the main list above a gray dividing line. Disable access to services by deselecting them in the Sharing preference pane.

- **Individual applications.** Turn access on or off for any application using the pop-up menu next to the program. You can also manually configure applications by clicking the Add (+) or Remove (–) buttons.

- **Automatically allow signed...** lets the firewall pass programs that have been verified by a third party to be legitimate. This includes software from Apple.

- **Enable stealth mode.** This option makes your computer ignore requests that are designed to check for the existence of a computer at a given address and which are often meant as probes for malicious intent.

Surf Safely

The most dangerous program on your computer is your Web browser. Criminals worldwide would like nothing better than to have you visit malicious sites, download and install software you shouldn't, and fool you into thinking you're viewing your bank's Web site instead of their bogus stand-in. Don't be fooled.

While OS X is resistant to common strategies that worked against Windows XP, the weakest link in your computer's security is, I'm afraid to say, you—and ne'er-do-wells know this. But you can easily avoid their lures by adhering to the following advice and using common sense.

Use a modern Web browser and keep it up to date

All the modern browsers for OS X are currently considered secure when all the security patches and updates have been installed. Some browsers release updates every few weeks.

If you're using a browser that's a year or two old, or if you haven't bothered to get the latest update, upgrade now (see Chapter 3 for details on upgrading software).

Don't install unfamiliar software

This may go without saying, but if a site offers you software with which you're unfamiliar, especially if you can't find reviews online—don't do it. (This is true for any software that someone emails you, too.) Evildoers rely on convincing you to launch and install software that causes harm.

Don't install custom video-player software

Several attacks have centered on software you allegedly need to install to view video in a format that QuickTime doesn't support. Don't install it.

Disable the "Open 'safe' files" option in Safari

If you use Safari, immediately open Safari's preferences and, in the General pane, deselect the option labeled "Open 'safe' files after downloading" (**Figure 10.12**). While Apple intended this feature to enhance security by disabling the automatic opening of "unsafe" files, exploits in the past have been based on hiding bad code in media and other file types.

Figure 10.12
The "safe" option isn't the smart option.

☐ Open "safe" files after downloading
  "Safe" files include movies, pictures, sounds,
  PDF and text documents, and archives.

Related to this is the "Automatically update safe downloads list" in the General section of the Security & Privacy preference pane. Apple regularly updates its file quarantine list to account for known malware (software designed to attack your computer when visiting the site). When such a file is downloaded, you're alerted that it's potentially dangerous and should be sent to the Trash.

Look for a green bar or highlighting for secure sites

A secure Web site shows a lock icon somewhere in the browser to indicate that your browser and the Web server have created an encrypted connection, and that the Web server is at the Internet address it claims. But many sites have gone one step further by employing Extended Validation (EV) secure certificates. An EV certificate is supposed to ensure that whatever firm set up the Web site has been vetted even further to validate its identity. The EV status is shown by a green bar or green highlighting in the Location field, where the URL appears (**Figure 10.13**, on the next page).

Figure 10.13
Clicking the EV indicator in Safari reveals more details on the site's identity.

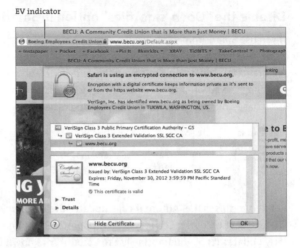

Most banks, credit unions, lending institutions, and credit card companies have paid slightly higher fees for this identity confirmation to reassure customers. If you visit a site of this kind and it lacks the green marker, but you've seen it there before, something's definitely wrong. And if a financial institution you deal with hasn't seen fit to go green, you should let them know that it matters.

Use OpenDNS to detect phishing sites

Phishing is the art of convincing you to visit a Web site that purports to be one you know but is actually run by a scammer. Phishing sites can be quite realistic, and they often employ domain names and other masking techniques that defuse your anxiety.

Fortunately, several firms have assembled and constantly update lists of Web pages and sites that are used as part of phishing attacks. They also often mark malicious sites that contain malware.

You can use one list of phishing sites to protect your surfing by changing a network setting to point to OpenDNS (www.opendns.com), a free provider of domain name service (DNS). (DNS is an Internet method of converting a human-readable name, like peachpit.com, into a numerical Internet address.) OpenDNS uses this list to identify and then block your access to these sites (**Figure 10.14**).

Figure 10.14
OpenDNS blocks and explains phishing sites.

To configure OpenDNS to provide domain lookups for your machine, do the following:

1. In the Network preference pane, select your network connection—the one with a green dot next to it—such as Ethernet or AirPort.

2. Click the Advanced button.

3. Click the DNS button at the top.

4. Under the DNS Servers area, click the Add (+) button and enter **208.67.222.222**. Then, click the Add (+) button again, and enter **208.67.220.220**. (You add two addresses for redundancy in case one server happens to be unavailable.)

5. Click OK.

6. Click Apply.

You can also set OpenDNS for an entire network if you use a gateway or base station (such as an AirPort Extreme) to provide network addresses via DHCP. In that device's setup program, enter the DNS server values listed in step 4.

Network Safely with Wi-Fi

The last piece of the personal security puzzle is protecting your computer when connecting to a network via Wi-Fi wireless networking. Wi-Fi is a weak link because signals travel through the air, and anyone with another computer and free software can intercept and view your data if it's not secured.

note Ethernet-connected computers and broadband networks are generally considered safe. Ethernet requires physical access—someone in your house or office—to break into. Broadband networks are generally well secured and monitored at the various network buildings through which data passes.

Use a VPN at hot spots

If you use your Mac at a Wi-Fi hot spot, such as a café, you need to secure your connection so data isn't sent without protection between your computer and the hot spot's Internet connection. A virtual private network (VPN) connection offers this option. VPNs create an encrypted tunnel between your computer and a server somewhere else on the Internet. This tunnel can't be penetrated with any known cracking software. Most corporations require roaming workers to use a VPN.

Individuals can "rent" a VPN connection from several firms. You can pay for access to publicVPN (publicvpn.com, $69.95 a year or $6.95 a month) and WiTopia (www.witopia.net, $49.99 to $69.99 a year).

Use Wi-Fi encryption

On your own network or one you manage, enable encryption and use a passphrase. For Apple's Wi-Fi base stations, either use the setup assistant when configuring the base station or follow these steps:

1. Launch AirPort Utility from the Utilities folder.

2. Select your base station to view information about its setup, and click the Edit button.

3. In the screen that appears, click the Wireless button.

4. From the Wireless Security pop-up menu, select WPA/WPA2 Personal if you have any Macs or Windows systems from 2004 or before, or WPA2 Personal if all computers were made after 2004.

5. Enter a password in the Wireless Password field, and re-enter it in the Verify Password field.

6. Click Update and wait for the base station to restart.

 The same password will work with Windows, iPhone, and all other devices with Wi-Fi sold in 2004 or later.

Anti-Virus Software

If you've come to the Mac from a Windows background, you know that any Windows-based PC needs a good anti-virus package. On the Mac, however, it's not needed. Seriously.

The Mac isn't immune to viruses and other malware, but so far there hasn't been a need to spend money and your computer's processing cycles toward anti-virus software. The best thing you can do right now is to stay abreast of security updates and follow news outlets such as TidBITS (tidbits.com, where I'm an editor).

11

Troubleshooting

With Apple's emphasis on making the Mac easy to use, it's easy to forget that under the crisp colors and soft drop shadows lies a complex bed of code that runs the show. No software is ever perfect, and although Apple has focused on improving performance and stability in Mountain Lion, bugs and other issues are sure to crop up.

This chapter is an introduction to troubleshooting problems, offering some general advice to help you locate and solve issues that might arise. I also provide specifics about repairing disk directory corruption, dealing with applications that frequently crash or refuse to operate, and working through network and connectivity issues.

General Troubleshooting

When something goes wrong on your Mac, it's often not clear what is causing the problem. The following is a list of general suggestions intended to narrow down the cause of the problem.

- **Restart the computer.** Applications can exhibit strange behavior when there isn't enough memory available for them to operate, which can happen if you've been running lots of applications for days or weeks. Or, perhaps a buggy program is interfering with other processes. Restarting the computer clears the caches and resets the environment.

- **Log in as a different user.** Remember in Chapter 2 when I recommended creating a test user account? Log out of your current account, then log in to the test one and see if the problem persists. If it's gone, then the culprit is some software running (most likely in the background) in your main user account. See "Other startup modes" later in this chapter to log in with startup items disabled.

- **Check cables and connections.** "Of course, *that* couldn't be it," I've said to myself on more than one occasion. And yet, after checking my hard disk for errors, running utilities, and restarting the computer, the problem has sometimes been a video or network cable that wasn't snug, or a bad FireWire or USB cable. Verify that all your connectors are tight. If the problem is with reading an external disk or connecting to a network, try a different cable.

- **Look online for more information.** It's possible other people are experiencing the same problem as you. Apple's support forums (discussions.apple.com) are a good place to start, as is a general Google search.

> **tip** My colleague Adam Engst wrote an article that presents a methodical approach to diagnosing computer problems. See "TidBITS Troubleshooting Primer," Part 1 (db.tidbits.com/article/6968) and Part 2 (db.tidbits.com/article/6975).

Troubleshoot Disk-Related Issues

OS X tracks the attributes of hundreds of thousands of files—not just where they're located on disk, but also what permissions apply to each one, how they interact with other files, and more. It does this efficiently, but sometimes the data can become corrupted by a bad installer, a buggy program, or, I'm convinced, gremlins.

Verify disk structure

OS X maintains a directory of your disk's file structure, which can get corrupted. The files themselves are usually perfectly fine, but the system has trouble locating them, which could lead to overwritten files if things get particularly bad. But it won't get that far, right? Because now you know what to do:

1. Launch Disk Utility, which is located in the Utilities folder within the Applications folder (or, in the Finder, choose Go > Utilities or press Command-Shift-U).

2. Select a volume in the left-hand pane and click the First Aid button at the top of the screen (**Figure 11.1**).

Figure 11.1
Disk Utility

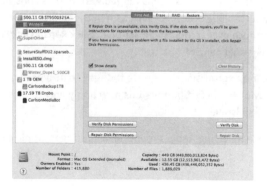

3. Click the Verify Disk button. A dialog informs you that the computer may be slow during the verification process; click Verify Disk to continue. Disk Utility scans the disk's directory and flags any problems.

4. If errors are found, Disk Utility can repair them, but it depends on which disk you're checking. The Repair Disk button is disabled if you're analyzing the startup disk. See "Start up from the Recovery OS" later in this chapter for instructions on how to repair the disk using the Recovery OS. If you've verified a non-startup disk, click Repair Disk to fix the errors.

5. After performing the repair, click Verify Disk again to make sure there are no other problems. If everything comes up green, you can quit Disk Utility.

tip Sometimes directory corruption is too severe for Disk Utility to repair. In that case, turn to Alsoft's DiskWarrior (alsoft.com), which succeeds where many other disk utilities fail.

Repair permissions

Every file on your hard disk is tagged with permissions that limit what actions can be performed, such as whether a file can be edited or not and which user accounts can act on it. Click Repair Disk Permissions in the First Aid pane of Disk Utility.

Repairing permissions was once thought to be a general fix for any weird behavior, but in fact permissions now apply only to files installed by Apple's installers.

See the following Apple support article: support.apple.com/kb/HT2963.

If an Application Crashes

When an application crashes, it usually occurs in one of two ways: the program disappears abruptly, or it becomes unresponsive. In the first case, you should see a dialog that gives you the option of sending a crash report to Apple (which is a good idea; no personal identifying data is sent along). Restart the application. If it crashes again, consider restarting the computer or using the general troubleshooting advice from earlier.

 note OS X uses protected memory, which means that when one application crashes, it doesn't bring down the rest of the machine.

Force quit

If the program is not responding, you'll probably also see the infamous SPOD—Spinning Pizza of Death (or SBOD, Spinning Beachball of Death), the rainbow-colored wheel that replaces the mouse pointer to indicate that OS X is busy processing something. In this case, try force-quitting the program using one of the following methods:

- Right-click (or control-click) the application's icon in the Dock and choose Force Quit (**Figure 11.2**). If the menu item reads just "Quit," hold the Option key to invoke the Force Quit option.

Figure 11.2
Force Quit from the Dock.

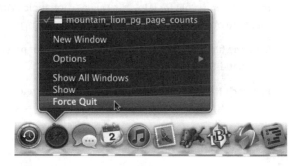

- If the Dock icon isn't working, go to the Apple menu and choose Force Quit, or press Command-Option-Esc. A dialog appears that shows running applications. Select one and click the Force Quit button.

- Open the Activity Monitor application (located in the Utilities folder), which reports on all of the running processes, including software running invisibly in the background. Select the dead program (listed in red) and click the Quit Process button.

Delete preferences

If a program is crashing repeatedly, try deleting its preferences file(s). Doing so under Mountain Lion is a bit more difficult than in versions earlier than Lion because Mountain Lion hides the user Library folder, where most application preferences files are stored. Here's how to access and delete them.

1. Quit the troublesome application if it's running.

2. In the Finder, hold the Option key and click the Go menu.

3. Choose the Libary menu item.

4. Open the Preferences folder.

5. Locate the preferences file belonging to your program—for example, the preferences file for iMovie is called "com.apple.iMovie.plist," and there are other "com.apple.iMovie" files (**Figure 11.3**).

6. Send the file(s) to the Trash (drag it to the Trash or press Command-Delete).

7. Relaunch the application. It will automatically create a new preferences file(s) set to the program's defaults.

Figure 11.3
Locating preferences files

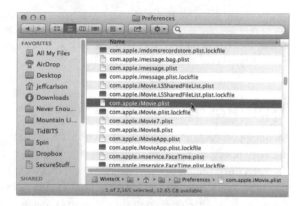

If You Can't Connect to the Internet

Web sites sometimes go offline and Internet service providers experience snags, but the difficulty could also be in your computer. Try these steps for regaining network access.

1. Open a new Safari window and attempt to access a Web page. If there's no connection, you'll see a warning.

2. Click the Network Diagnostics button on that warning page to launch a utility of the same name.

3. Choose an interface for connecting to the Internet and click Continue.

4. Follow the rest of the instructions provided by Network Diagnostics (which vary depending on the nature of the problem).

 Is your Mac regularly connecting to the wrong network interface? For example, your MacBook Pro is plugged into Ethernet at your office, but it's actually getting network access via AirPort. You can choose which services have priority over others. In the Network preference pane, click the Action menu (the gear icon) below the list of interfaces and choose Set Service Order. In the dialog that appears, drag the services to change their order, with the highest-priority interface at the top; click OK to exit. OS X will then use your preferred network type first.

Troubleshoot at Startup

Mountain Lion doesn't come on a disc, which is an issue if you need to start up your computer using something other than your Mac's internal hard disk (for example, to repair the disk using Disk Utility). As an alternative, Mountain Lion creates a hidden partition during installation called Recovery OS that can start up the machine and provide diagnostic utilities.

Start up from the Recovery OS

To access the tools on the Recovery OS, do the following:

1. Restart the computer and hold Command-R; or, hold the Option key and choose Recovery from the row of startup volumes.

2. Choose one of the following options from the OS X Utilities window that appears, and then click Continue:

   - **Restore from a Time Machine Backup.** Make sure your Time Machine disk is connected and follow the instructions.

   - **Reinstall OS X.** This option installs a fresh copy of Mountain Lion. Part of the process involves re-downloading the Mountain Lion installer, however, so make sure you're online and have a robust connection that can download the 4 GB file.

   - **Get Help Online.** Choose this option to open Safari and view support documents. To access the Internet, make sure your computer is connected via Ethernet or Wi-Fi; you can choose a wireless network from the Wi-Fi menu in the upper-right corner of the screen.

- **Disk Utility.** Open Disk Utility to diagnose, repair, or format a disk.

3. To exit the tools and restart your computer, quit OS X Utilities.

tip If you've enabled FileVault on your Mac, you won't be able to access the Recovery OS by holding the Option key—the login screen is the first thing to appear (it needs your password to access the rest of the initialization sequence). Instead, try restarting with Command-R held down. If that doesn't work, do this: At the login screen...do nothing for a few minutes. A message will appear that begins, "If you're having a problem entering your password..." Now, press and hold the Mac's power button to shut it down. Wait a few seconds, and then press the button (a normal press, no need to hold it) to start up the computer. The OS X Utilities window will appear.

Other startup modes

The Recovery OS isn't the only way to start up the Mac when you suspect something is wrong. Here are other helpful modes.

- **Choose a startup disk.** If you have multiple disks that can run the computer (including a Boot Camp partition running Windows), hold Option at startup to display icons for each disk. Double-click one to start up from it.

- **Start up in Target Disk mode.** With two Macs connected via FireWire or Thunderbolt, you can run one as if it were just an external drive. This is a good way to run Disk Utility on a startup disk if you can't access the Recovery OS. Press and hold the T key during startup until you see a large FireWire icon.

- **Start up from a CD or DVD.** To force the Mac to use an inserted CD or DVD as the startup disk, hold the C key during startup.

- **Eject a disk at startup.** Do you have a recalcitrant disc that won't come out of your Mac's media drive? Unless it's physically jammed in there, restart your computer and hold the mouse button (or trackpad button) during startup to force the drive's eject mechanism.

- **Start up with login items disabled.** This technique is good for trouble-shooting whether a background process is interfering with some other software. Hold Shift as you start up to boot into a safe mode.

- **Start up in single-user mode.** If you're having problems even getting to the login stage, hold Command-S during startup to boot into single-user mode. This is a bare-bones, text-only mode that accepts Unix commands. At the command prompt, type:

  /sbin/fsck -fy

  That command performs a disk check as if you were running Disk Utility. Single-user mode is really designed for programmers or for troubleshooting problems that may be interfering with Mountain Lion's startup process.

  When the disk check is finished and you have another command prompt, type:

  reboot

Support Resources

Remember, there's a lot of help out there if you need it.

- **Apple Support:** www.apple.com/support/

- **Apple Support discussions:** discussions.apple.com

- **Apple retail stores:** www.apple.com/retail/
  (Schedule a free appointment with an Apple Genius.)

- **Apple phone support:**

  USA: 1-800-APL-CARE (1-800-275-2273)

  Canada: 1-800-263-3394

  Worldwide: www.apple.com/support/contact/phone_contacts.html

- **Apple Consultants Network:** consultants.apple.com

Should You Purchase AppleCare?

I get this question whenever Apple releases new computers. When you buy a new Mac, you get one year of AppleCare, Apple's warranty service. It doesn't cover accidents like dropping a MacBook Pro onto the floor, but it does address things like a faulty logic board. You can extend that warranty to three years from the date you purchased the computer by buying AppleCare as an extended warranty.

I normally hate extended warranties—they always seem like they're designed to rip you off. And yet, nearly all of my Macs have benefitted from having AppleCare beyond the one-year warranty period. So my general advice is to purchase AppleCare for laptops but not desktops, since laptops tend to have smaller, more sensitive electronics and are transported more often. If you are going to buy AppleCare, you must do it before the first year warranty expires.

Index

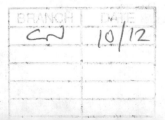